FARIDA KHALAF

FARIDA and her brothers were brought up in the Yazidi community in Kocho, Iraq. She was 19 years old when ISIS attacked her village, killed the men, captured the women and sold them into slavery. After four months, Farida managed to escape against all odds. She was reunited with her mother and her brothers in an Iraqi refugee camp and was granted asylum in Germany in 2015.

ANDREA C. HOFFMANN is a Middle East expert, a writer for *Focus* magazine in Germany, and author of numerous books. Her specialisation is the situation of women in Muslim countries.

FARIDA KHALAF
WITH ANDREA C. HOFFMANN

The Girl Who Escaped ISIS

Farida's Story

Translated from the German by
Jamie Bulloch

VINTAGE

1 3 5 7 9 10 8 6 4 2

Vintage
20 Vauxhall Bridge Road,
London SW1V 2SA

Vintage is part of the Penguin Random House group of companies
whose addresses can be found at global.penguinrandomhouse.com

Penguin
Random House
UK

First published in Vintage in 2017
First published in hardback by Square Peg in 2016

www.vintage-books.co.uk

A CIP catalogue record for this book is available from the British Library

ISBN 9781784702755

This book has been selected to receive financial assistance from English PEN's
"PEN Translates!" programme, supported by Arts Council England. English
PEN exists to promote literature and our understanding of it, to uphold
writers' freedoms around the world, to campaign against the persecution and
imprisonment of writers for stating their views, and to promote the friendly
co-operation of writers and the free exchange of ideas. www.englishpen.org

Supported using public funding by
ARTS COUNCIL ENGLAND · ENGLISH PEN

Printed and bound by Clays Ltd, St Ives Plc

Penguin Random House is committed to a sustainable future
for our business, our readers and our planet. This book is
made from Forest Stewardship Council® certified paper.

MIX
Paper from
responsible sources
FSC® C018179

AUTHOR'S NOTE

My name is Farida Khalaf, it is real. However, the names of all the other people who appear in this book have been changed. Only names of people in public life are real.

CONTENTS

PROLOGUE

My father showed me how to stand. 'Put your left foot a touch further forward and bend your legs slightly.'

He corrected my posture by taking hold of my shoulders from behind and adjusting my torso so I was front on. As a border guard in the Iraqi army he knew how to handle rifles. He placed the gun, an AK-47, in my hands. The Kalashnikov wasn't as heavy as I'd anticipated.

'Put your right hand at the back by the trigger,' he said. 'Like that. Now with your left hand you can align the barrel at the front. Aim at the tree trunk over there.' I got one of the mulberry trees in our garden in my sights. 'And fire!'

I tentatively fingered the trigger. Nothing happened.

'Go on,' he said. 'Don't be afraid, Farida.'

I pulled the metal lever gently until finally it clicked quietly. From behind me Dad laughed.

'Just like that,' he said. 'Well done!'

I looked at him quizzically.

'I haven't taken off the safety catch. But we'll change that right away. This is how you do it.' He showed me how to release the safety catch on the right-hand side of the receiver. 'Are you ready?'

'Of course,' I said, focused.

'Careful, now.'

'OK.'

'Are you aiming right?'

I nodded.

'Go on then.'

A loud report echoed through our garden and the force of the Kalashnikov had me staggering.

'Bravo!' Dad said, grinning beneath his dark moustache.

The two of us walked over to the tree, to examine the results of my first shooting attempt. And, in the event, a small piece of metal was lodged at the very right-hand edge of the trunk. The empty cartridge lay in the dust about a metre away.

'You've got talent,' my father said. 'With a little practice you'll be better than your mother.'

'Do you think so?' I asked excitedly. He stroked my head with affection.

'Yes, you've just got to do it a few times, then it'll be a piece of cake. I'll put up a target for you in the garden. You'll see, over time you'll lose that fear of the bang and you'll be better at offsetting the kick.'

I nodded eagerly. I was terribly proud that my father was teaching me, at the age of fifteen, how to handle a Kalashnikov. He'd already shown my mother and my brother Delan, who was a couple of years older than me, how to do it years ago. Although not my brother Serhad, who was two years younger. It was a sure sign that he thought I was grown up enough to defend our house and property should it ever come to that.

There were three rifles in a box in my parents' bedroom. One was Dad's army service rifle; the others he'd picked up at the bazaar.

'Women need to know how to use a weapon too,' he said. 'When I've got enough money I'll buy another AK-47 so that there's one for each of us in an emergency.'

Dad didn't specify what this emergency might be. And I didn't have the imagination to picture it. Back then it didn't cross my mind that my father's circumspection might be linked to the fact that we were Yazidis and not Muslims. I was just thinking of burglars who might try to steal our valuables. I was only fifteen years old and the catastrophe awaiting us in the future was completely beyond my imagination.

1

OUR WORLD AS IT ONCE WAS

We lived in Kocho, a village on the plain to the south of Mount Sinjar in northern Iraq. It had 1,700 inhabitants. In spring the countryside is ablaze with all the colours of the rainbow. Around the village the many trees and plants come into bloom, as well as grasses on which the shepherds drive their goats. In summer the heat dries everything out and the plants wither. Because of this the villagers had created a few ponds around Kocho, from which we irrigated our fields. Every day we had to water our garden too, which was surrounded by a high wall. This was one of my chores. Mornings and evenings I would take the long hose, turn on the tap on the terrace and spray all our plants.

We had a very beautiful garden in which mulberry, almond and apricot trees grew. And in their shade the vegetables that my mother planted thrived too: courgettes, leeks, aubergines, potatoes, onions, salad and heads of cabbage. Around the terrace a variety of roses flowered, giving off a beguiling aroma, especially in the evenings. In the hot season my mother, my younger brothers Serhad, Shivan, Keniwar and I would spend almost our entire time in this little paradise. My father and my elder brother Delan enjoyed the peace and fresh air here too, when they weren't working.

The house itself was on one floor and had five rooms: a kitchen, a living room, my parents' bedroom, a bedroom for my four brothers – and one for me. As the sole daughter of the family I was entitled to my own little realm. Despite this I often regretted having no sisters, with whom I would gladly have shared my room. I was, however, allowed to invite friends back as often as I liked. My friend Evin and my best friend Nura were regular visitors to our house. Nura and I were eighteen now, and in our final year at school, and I was excited to consider what life might have in store for me next. Evin, on the other hand, was a few years older than us and had long since finished school. We envied all the free time she had; we frequently had to spend long afternoons doing our homework, while she helped her female relatives with odd chores around the house, and looked forward to being married off. Her greatest dream was to become a housewife with lots of children. With her calm, even temper Evin was like an elder sister to Nura and me.

Of my brothers, I liked Delan the best. We hung around together and shared many interests. In the afternoons we loved playing football in the garden. My big brother also secretly taught me how to drive in the mountains. Dad had only taught him and Serhad, as he didn't think women needed to know how. In any case it was unusual for people in our village to have driving lessons or take the test.

Our house was supposed to have two floors. Well, that's what my father's original plan had been when he built it with my uncle. But the money he'd set aside soon ran out. With a soldier's salary and a bit extra from farming he didn't have that much leeway. What's more, Dad was insistent that all his children should go to school. In short, there was always something more important to shell out for than a second storey. And over time we got used to the metal rods and wires sticking up out of the roof. Lots of houses in Kocho looked like this. The rods were a sign that another floor could be built on top at any time. And in summer, when it was too hot to sleep in the house, we would go up to the roof with our mats to enjoy the fresh night air up there.

Taking a pragmatic view of the situation, my mother tied lines between the rods and started hanging her washing up on the roof. This came as great relief to Delan and me, who'd often been hauled over the coals when our dirty football missed the goal and landed in some clean sheets that were drying in the garden.

For some time now, however, a concrete mixer and sacks of cement had stood amid the rods. Delan had bought these out of his pay as a builder. The reason was that my brother wanted to marry. And for this, of course, he needed an apartment he could move into with his wife.

He also needed a wife. On one of our jaunts to the mountains he'd admitted to me that the girl he'd originally been in love with had been forced to turn him down. Unfortunately her parents had already promised her to another man and there was nothing to be done about it. Now Delan was trying to court Zevin, a cousin of ours who I was very fond of.

'I'll pray that her parents accept you,' I promised him solemnly.

The neighbouring villages were mainly populated by Muslim Arabs. They were different from us in every way, not just because of their religion. They had other customs and traditions too. We spoke Kurdish, they spoke Arabic. And as we Yazidis only marry within our own religious group, we had no relatives in these villages either. We did, however, maintain friendly and above all commercial relations with the Muslims. Muslim traders would often come to Kocho to sell their fruit or sweets. Of course the children were delighted to welcome these salesmen, and the adults were very pleased with their wares too.

Every boy in our village, moreover, had a Muslim 'godfather' – the man who holds the little baby in his arms during the circumcision ceremony. Usually the entire village comes to watch this ritual. When my youngest brother Keniwar was circumcised, for example, he was held by a Muslim friend of my father's. Through this he became Keniwar's 'uncle', his protector. Even if there were no blood connections between the families, the Muslim godfather would undertake an obligation to help the boy, and later the man, whenever he needed his support. At the same time the act strengthened the bonds between the Yazidi and Muslim families, and so also between my father and his friend of a different faith.

But in spite of such alliances, we Yazidis had an extremely dubious reputation among Muslims. And we knew it too. For they didn't try particularly hard to conceal what they thought of us. When they visited the village they refused to eat our food, afraid it might be 'unclean'. As we place great emphasis on hospitality, we regarded this as an affront. For a long time as a child I couldn't understand why they thought of us in this way.

But the elders in the village explained that it had always been thus.

'Our history is one of persecution and suffering,' my grandfather told me. My father's father lived next door to us, as is usual in our culture. He was a dignified old gentleman with a white moustache and he habitually wore the traditional white robes, which for us indicate spiritual purity. 'They've all persecuted us: the Muslim Kurds, the Iranian Shah's governors and the Ottoman sultans. They massacred and butchered us on seventy-two occasions. How many times have they stolen our women, driven us from our homeland, forced us with raised swords to renounce our religion?'

Grandad stroked my head with his large, coarse hand while I listened to these gruesome stories from the past. 'Beware these people, my little one,' he said, 'for they call us *abadat al-shaytan*: those who worship the Lord of Hell.'

Now I got a proper fright. 'But why?'

'Because somebody concocted this lie a long, long time ago,' he replied. Grandad looked at me. Like his hair, his eyes appeared to be covered in a grey veil. It seemed as if he were weighing up whether I was old enough to understand things. 'It's a complicated story – you'll find out soon enough.'

The religious rituals in our village were inseparable from the cycles of nature. Every morning before it got light I'd climb up to the roof with my parents and siblings to greet the first rays of the sun. Sometimes, when it was cold, we'd stay in the house and stand in the spot where it first shone in. We would turn our heads to the sun and open out our palms, similar to how Muslims and Christians do when they pray. Then we'd put our hands together and say, 'Amen, amen, amen. May our religion be blessed. God will help our religion to survive.' We Yazidis do not pray to the sun, however. In our prayers we always address God. We only venerate the sun in the same way that we venerate the moon and Venus, because divine energy flows through them. Several times during the day and once at night we worship God in the face of these heavenly bodies.

Light, particularly sunlight, is very important in our faith. After all, everything in the world depends on the sun, doesn't it? Could a plant flourish without light? Could we cultivate our fields? Could we harvest and satisfy our hunger with the yield? No! This is why the sun is sacred to us; its light is our place of worship and our most important connection to God.

The various seasons are also linked to religious festivals in our culture. In Kocho the ritual cycle began with the festival *Sere Sal*, after the start of the new year at the end of March, which we would celebrate on the first Wednesday in April – 'Red Wednesday'. On this day we used to decorate our house with flowers and paint eggs in bright colours, as in our way of thinking they stand for the rebirth of all life and the beginning of the world. As a child I would hunt for the eggs in the garden, and later my mother and other women from the village would offer these same eggs to our ancestors at the cemetery as a feast.

We celebrated *Cle Havine*, the 'Forty Days of Summer', and *Cle Zivistane*, the 'Forty Days of Winter'. Both festivals came with elaborate religious ceremonies, ending with a three-day fast.

The most important event of the year, though, was the pilgrimage to Lalish. In autumn, when the intense heat of the summer had abated and the weather was pleasantly mild again, the whole village would make its way to this mystical place, a wonderful green valley irrigated by two springs that we hold to be sacred. It is about 150 kilometres north-east of Kocho, in the mountains between Dohuk and Mosul.

For me, Lalish represents something like a second home, a spiritual one, as from the cradle my parents took me on the annual journey to the valley. Even as a baby I bathed in the waters of the white spring. Lalish is a divine place for us.

Like all the men in the village, for this solemn occasion my father would swap his blue army uniform, which he loved wearing, for a white robe and a white scarf on his head, which he tied in the Arab style with a black headband. My mother would also wrap a white scarf around her head. Unlike Muslim women, Yazidis are not obliged to veil themselves. So the other girls and I would go without covering our heads, and our clothes for the pilgrimage would be relatively modern. We wore the same trousers, skirts and blouses we went to school in. But we would always make sure that at least one item of clothing was white.

Each year, when we turned into the valley, my father would order us to take off our shoes and continue barefoot. Nobody was to dirty the sacred earth with the soles of their shoes. 'Do not forget that no less a being than Sheikh Adi walked upon this ground,' he reminded us.

Sheikh Adi, a preacher who lived in Lalish many centuries ago, is worshipped by us. His grave is in the sanctuary which lies at one of the valley's gently sloping hillsides. You can see from afar the sand-coloured complex with the pointed towers of the holy graves.

We would seek out a spot near the shrine and unload our bundles. The guest houses were reserved for very important people and members of our priestly caste. Normal people like us set up camp outside. We would bring a large covering that my brothers tied to four wooden posts. This served as both a sunshade and protection against the rain. We also stored our crockery, blankets and food beneath this improvised tent roof. We tied a goat, which we'd brought along for food, to a nearby tree.

I loved our time in Lalish. For us young people this autumn week chiefly meant holiday and a great deal of fun. It was like a massive camping trip with all your friends and relatives.

I'd spend the days with my family. Each day would have a specific schedule. On the first we would wander to the Silat Bridge at the lower end of the valley. It marks the crossing point between Lalish's earthly and heavenly realms. We'd wash our hands three times in the water under the bridge and three times we'd cross the bridge with torches in our hands, saying, 'The Silat Bridge, on one side is Hell, on the other Paradise.' Then we'd go to the upper part of the valley and sing hymns. We repeated this procedure for three days.

The bull sacrifice on the fifth day was one of the high points. The deafening salvoes that announced its death made all the men hurry to the sanctuary. My father and brothers didn't want to miss the spectacle either. We women were less keen, however. 'I only have to smell all that blood to be sick,' my mother confided in me.

What I loved most of all about Lalish were the evenings, when there was traditional dancing. Seven men, swathed entirely in white clothes, ceremoniously danced twice around the sun symbol to the music of the Qewels, the holy singers who preserve our religious knowledge. They followed a fakir, a holy ascetic, who wore a dark fur and a pointed black hat. I found this ritual, which lasted all evening, both mysterious and fascinating.

I'd often slip away with Nura and Evin to meet our friends under the cover of darkness. Because of course we preferred to spend our time with people our own age rather than with our families. Sometimes we got to meet children from other villages further north from Kocho this way too. The adults frowned upon this, because they were afraid of illicit friendships between the members of the two sexes. But in the overall chaos and euphoria of the pilgrimage they couldn't prevent contact altogether.

These encounters were invariably harmless in the end. After all, my friends and I had been brought up strictly according to our community's code of honour, in which a bride's virginity plays an extremely important role. For us, premarital relationships were out of the question. So it never got any further than us teasing the boys of our own age or at most exchanging stolen glances.

2

ONE FINAL WONDERFUL SUMMER

At school they called me 'calculator'. My maths teacher gave this nickname to me because I was the cleverest in the class at this subject. Whenever Mr Siamand set us a problem and none of my classmates could solve it, he would finally turn to me. 'So, Farida, what do you think?' he asked. 'Would you show the others how to do it?'

'Of course,' I replied, striding confidently towards the blackboard. With a stick of chalk I wrote up the individual stages in solving the problem, while explaining long-windedly how to get from one stage to the next. Behind me I could hear my classmates grumbling. They were annoyed that I was better at maths than them, especially the boys.

'What's going on? Farida's not our teacher!' they complained. Their voices oozed envy. But Mr Siamand always came to my defence. 'Just concentrate and listen to how Farida works out the answer,' he advised them. 'She's a wonderful teacher. You know, she's even better at maths than I am.'

Each time I would turn bright red. Of course I was delighted by the praise issuing from the mouth of my teacher. But to be honest I don't have to try that hard at maths. I love this subject; everything's so clear, so structured, so logical. It seems strange to me that someone can't understand this beautiful, ordered world. I find it all so simple.

I was particularly good at exponentiation, which we were learning in spring 2014. While my classmates frowned and chewed their pencils as they struggled to work out the answers, I saw them in my head in a flash. My classmates thought it was magic, but I just found it pretty satisfying.

Physics was my second favourite subject. I found this easy too. But unfortunately our physics teacher, Mr Khalil, explained everything in such a dull and laborious way. When he came into our classroom after the maths lesson I would lay my head on the desk and groan to Nura, 'I'm going to have a kip. Wake me up when he's finished.'

She would giggle and sweep her long brown hair from her face. With her light skin and button nose Nura was by far the most beautiful girl in our class. But unlike me she really struggled in both subjects. Occasionally when she was sweating over some problem or other, she'd look over at me in despair. 'How on earth do you do this?' she whispered. 'Have you got a calculator there?'

'No!' I assured her. 'If you come by this afternoon I'll explain it to you.'

Of course, studying together was just a pretext for us. I was always delighted when Nura came to visit. My mother was pleased too. As my father worked shifts – and would regularly be detailed to the Syrian border for ten days at a time – we women felt alone and occasionally very lonely. In our society, moreover, we believe that guests bring a blessing to the house.

So after school we went up to the roof with our maths books and buried ourselves in the units we'd studied in the morning. I tried my best to help Nura grasp the secrets of maths and physics, but the stuff would not stick in her head. It seemed as if the light breeze drifting over to us from Mount Sinjar carried my words away before they got to Nura. I blinked in the sun and listened to the tweeting of the birds in our garden. In truth it was really too nice a day to waste on studying.

'Come on, let's have a break,' I suggested.

Nura agreed at once. We closed our books and went down into the garden together. From the kitchen I fetched a carafe of lemonade that my mother had made freshly that morning. I poured us each a glass and decorated it with mint leaves that grew in our garden and smelled wonderful.

'Studying makes you hungry,' I said to Nura with a wink. She laughed. We always used this as an excuse when we were caught on a kitchen raid. Both of us adored snacking and, irrespective of whether we were at her house or mine, we'd plunder the fridge or harvest whatever delicacies the garden had to offer.

Nura particularly loved our raspberries, which glowed in soft hues. 'Your roses are even more beautiful this year,' she said.

'Yes,' I replied proudly. 'But have you seen our lilies?' I pointed to the precious blooms that grew in the widest array of colours. Nura sniffed them and gently stroked a petal.

'They're really extraordinary,' she had to admit. I broke off a yellow flower and placed it in her maths book. 'So you'll be able to do the next test blindfolded,' I promised her.

She plucked a flower too and put it in my book. 'Even if you don't need it, it'll remind you of me.'

At that moment I heard my mother's footsteps behind us. A checked scarf was tied around her head and she was carrying a mattock. She must have been weeding in the vegetable patch behind our house. 'You two aren't thieving again, are you?' she asked. We held our maths books up to our chests and shook our heads in sync.

My mother eyed us suspiciously. She knew how much we enjoyed giving each other flowers. But she couldn't convict us of any crime. 'You should at least give them a chance to grow,' she said, to be on the safe side.

We looked indignant. 'But that's what we're doing!'

Shortly before the summer holidays a maths teacher from another village came to our school. Mr Ahmed was responsible for examining us. He was a vertically challenged, bearded and very portly man, who had a reputation for being particularly hard to please. And he took pains to convey this impression. 'If just one of you in this class manages to get 70 per cent in my test then you're not so bad,' he bragged.

Along with his tests, Mr Ahmed arrived in our village with a whole host of prejudices too. Like so many Muslims, he probably thought that we Yazidis were completely uneducated because we lived here in such isolation.

All my classmates quivered in awe. Nura's face was as white as a sheet. But I pretended to be unimpressed. 'What are you talking about? I'm brilliant at maths. Of course I'll get more than 70 per cent.'

Mr Ahmed looked at me in amazement. 'Hmm, you seem to be very sure of yourself,' was his not very friendly reply. 'But we'll soon find out how good you actually are.'

He collected our maths books so no one could cheat. When Nura held out her book the pressed lily fell on the floor. The colour of my friend's face turned from white to bright red. She hurriedly picked the flower up and put it on the desk. I took the flower she'd given me from my book, too, before handing it in, and placed it right beside hers. 'Nothing can go wrong now,' I whispered to Nura.

Mr Ahmed handed out the test. 'It's really very difficult. So don't fret if you can't manage it,' he reiterated. He did seem to think we were idiots.

I was determined to prove the contrary. Focusing myself, I got stuck into the questions. Obviously the format of the test was somewhat different from the ones Mr Siamand set us. But all the same it was far from impossible. He really hadn't concocted anything devilish. I worked everything out and then checked my answers. A sideways glance revealed that Nura was, as usual, struggling with the questions. I tried to arrange the sheet of paper with my answers on it in such a way that she might be able to take a peek. But Mr Ahmed's eyes were vigilant. He'd already noticed that I'd stopped working. 'Well, well, given up already?' he sneered.

'Absolutely not. I've finished.'

He raised his eyebrows in surprise. 'You can hand your paper in, then,' he said, and ordered me out of the room. Nura followed soon afterwards.

We waited anxiously for the results. A few days later Mr Ahmed returned our marked papers. He grinned beneath his beard as he handed mine back. I found this hard to gauge – was his smile malicious or benign? There were lots of red ticks on my paper. Right at the bottom he'd scribbled my mark: 99 per cent. My heart leapt for joy. Nura had actually managed to do a third of the questions – and she passed too.

After the lesson Mr Ahmed beckoned me over again. 'I've seldom encountered a maths genius like you,' he told me. 'Have you ever considered becoming a maths teacher when you're older?'

'That would be my absolute dream,' I stammered in delight. 'Do you think it might be a possibility?'

'Of course. Mr Siamand or I could nominate you for a grant.'

I nodded enthusiastically. What a fantastic suggestion! I considered it a great distinction that this strict teacher thought me capable of becoming a maths teacher myself. No one in my family had become anything like that before.

I come from a modest background. My ancestors were small farmers and had never received any sort of formal education, as we belong to the lowest of the three Yazidi castes. Among the older generation, even learning how to read and write had been frowned upon. Hymns and prayers were simply passed down orally from our sheikhs and pirs. It only changed in 1970, when Saddam Hussein introduced compulsory school education. After this a school was built in Kocho too. But the teachers had always come from outside – until now. Would I, perhaps, be the first person to become a teacher in my own village?

I hurried home as proud as a peacock, looking forward to telling my parents the good news. This summer was going to be terrific, I thought, throwing my head back and shouting with sheer delight. Life was being kind to me.

*

In the holidays, things proceeded at a leisurely pace at home. I relaxed, had long lie-ins and met up with Nura and Evin. We'd organise picnics, browse fashion catalogues together and dress each other's long brown hair, pinning it into elaborate updos. We would keep our hair like this all day until one of our mothers put her foot down. 'Farida, untie that bun and give your hair a good brush!' my mother might remonstrate. 'Or are you going to wait until you're infested with lice? You'll bring bugs into this house!' I'd grumble as I brushed out my hair and bid goodbye to my dream of not only being the first maths teacher in my village, but also the most elegant.

I was helping Mum with the housework as well. As a daughter this was my duty, but I enjoyed it and didn't consider it too much of an effort to lend a hand with cleaning, washing, chopping wood or weeding.

But most of all I loved cooking for the family. Mum began teaching me at a young age how to prepare a variety of dishes, so that later on my husband would be pleased with me, as she put it. I was particularly good at making a local dish we call *kamalles*, fried chamomile flowers. And my kebab of fresh lamb was also famous – in the family, at least. When the spit sizzled over an open fire its enticing aroma wafted through the entire house, making everyone salivate. My four brothers would buzz around me like pesky flies and could barely wait for me to announce, 'It's ready!'

Unfortunately, our father didn't spend as much time with us as usual that summer. All the soldiers along the 605-kilometre border with our neighbour Syria had to do extra shifts, as the situation was tense due to the civil war raging there. Over the past two years Sunni terrorist groups had conquered large swathes of northern Syria. The central government of President Bashar al-Assad now only controlled the area around Damascus. The Islamists, who had seized power in the north, were forcing the population to follow strict Islamic codes of behaviour, while also hunting down all Christians and those of other faiths.

The most successful and brutal of these terrorist groups was an organisation called al-Dawla al-Islamiya fil Iraq wa'al Sham – Islamic State of Iraq and Syria – or Daesh for short. In Europe the abbreviation ISIS or IS is more common. These terrorists had more money and better weapons than all the other Islamists. In the past few months they had conquered many cities on the other side of the border. Large numbers of Shias, Christians, Druze and Alawites tried to flee their rule of terror, otherwise they risked being killed.

'It pains me terribly to have to send these people away,' I heard my father despondently tell my mother on one occasion when he was at home briefly. 'These fanatics show no sympathy to them.'

'Isn't it our duty to help them?' she asked.

'We have to be very careful,' he replied. 'ISIS has grand plans. Some of these supposed refugees are their Trojan horses. It's their job to start new terror cells in Iraqi cities.'

'Do they intend to seize power here too?'

'They certainly would if they could. They want to bring the whole of the Middle East under their control and here in Iraq they've put out feelers. They're already established in Fallujah and Ramadi. And apparently they've also got sympathisers in Mosul among former Saddam loyalists.'

My mother shook herself, as if to shoo away an ominous feeling. 'Who on earth are these people?'

My father sighed. 'The same lot who made our lives hell during the American occupation. Remember al-Zarqawi, who carried out bomb attacks and murdered Shias and Christians a few years back?'

'Yes,' my mother said – even I knew him, his name was well known and infamous in Iraq. 'He was the former al-Qaeda chief in Iraq, wasn't he? Didn't he die some time ago?'

'He did,' my father confirmed. 'But he has a successor, Abu Bakr al-Baghdadi. And he's every bit as brutal as his predecessor. This man comes from Samarra in southern Iraq and he spent five years rotting in an American military prison. His movement was as good as dead when the Americans pulled their troops out. But then the civil war broke out in Syria and al-Baghdadi sent the few remaining militias to the battlefield on the other side of the border. There they and other jihadis were given support by the Gulf States, Saudi Arabia and Qatar in particular. But Turkey sent weapons too, because they wanted to topple al-Assad and strengthen the radical Sunnis in the country. And they succeeded! Today al-Baghdadi's men wield more influence than all the other groups in Syria. They're battle-seasoned and just swimming in money and arms. That's why they're so dangerous.'

'But not for us, surely?' my mother asked anxiously.

'No,' my father laughed nervously. 'It may be different in the south, but here they don't have a chance – my colleagues and I will make sure they don't come over.'

My mother fell silent; she didn't seem entirely convinced.

'Or do you think that 350,000 armed men can't deal with a small bunch of terrorists?' my father said to reassure her.

I was surprised by the undertone of concern in my parents' conversation. It had never occurred to me before that jihadis could pose a threat to us in the village. The Syrian–Iraqi border that my father guarded was only about fifty kilometres from Kocho. But these were light years for me. I'd never been to Syria. And the civil war there was taking place on television, far beyond my own reality and my everyday life.

This began to change when the flashpoints got closer. 'Have you heard?' Nura asked just as Evin and I were coming into the house from the garden to deposit our apricot harvest in the kitchen. 'What do you mean?' I said, carefully flapping my left hand to shoo away a pesky bee, which was showing an interest in our fruit. We were planning to make jam from the sweet apricots today. But our friend was fixated on the television in the sitting room, and had put her bowl down on the floor. 'Turn it up a bit,' she instructed my little brother Keniwar.

The news was on. 'The Golden Guard has flown in helicopters to the city,' I heard the newsreader say. The camera showed soldiers leaping from Iraqi helicopters, dressed entirely in black. The elite forces of the Iraqi army were carrying machine guns.

'What's happened?' I asked.

'Shh,' Nura said, staring in concentration at the screen.

The footage was from Samarra in the Iraqi province of Salahuddin, which is in fact a Sunni metropolis, but it houses one of the most important Shia shrines. Trouble had often broken out there in the past between Shias and Sunnis. So at first I suspected that Sunnis might have attacked the shrine. But from what the newsreader was saying, I gathered that a convoy of vehicles carrying heavily armed terrorists had invaded the city that morning. Now the soldiers were trying to retake control of Samarra. There was probably already a number of killed and wounded on both sides.

'I hope nothing's happened to my cousin,' Nura whispered. 'They only recently transferred Ibrahim to Samarra.'

Evin and I looked anxiously at Nura. We could well understand her unease. As working for the Iraqi security forces was a much sought-after job among Yazidis, almost all of us had relatives in the army. And I was also afraid that the terrorists might attack the border posts and something would happen to my father. Over the last few weeks and months there had been several attacks and skirmishes there with jihadis. It seemed as if the area controlled by the Syrian terrorists was not big enough for them. As if they were determined to carry the conflict over to our side of the border too.

'Why don't we go and see your aunt?' I suggested. 'Maybe she knows more about it.'

'And maybe she knows absolutely nothing,' Nura said, by which she meant the onslaught itself. 'If she's heard nothing about it, we'd only be worrying her unnecessarily. If something *has* happened to Ibrahim, we'll find out soon enough.'

'Better not upset her,' Evin agreed.

We left the television on in the sitting room and went back to the kitchen to wash and stone the apricots. Some we cut into small pieces, sprinkled with sugar and put them in the fridge to have later for dessert. But most of them ended up in a large cooking pot, which we heated on a gas flame with kilos of sugar. The combination gave off a tantalisingly sweet and fruity smell, which became more intense the longer it simmered away. It was going to be a wonderful jam.

On television they reported the latest developments. In Baquba, north-east of Baghdad, a car bomb had exploded. And in Ramadi, the capital of Iraq's Anbar province, where ISIS was well established, their fighters had occupied the university campus. Although the newsreader tried not to make the events sound too dramatic, the fact was that the terrorists had taken hundreds of students hostage.

'That's unbelievable,' I said to Evin – and decided there and then that, if the grant worked out, I wouldn't study maths anywhere but in the Kurdish area. Maybe in Sinjar or Dohuk, where distant relations of ours lived. The Sunni south was definitely too unsafe for me. I could see that now.

Over the course of the afternoon – we were already filling preserving jars with our jam – the situation eased somewhat. The students in Ramadi were set free. And the army was able to take back Samarra. We gave a sigh of relief. At least the jihadis wouldn't be able to establish themselves permanently in that city as well. I found it worrying enough that they'd managed to take possession of it so quickly. I was anxious to find out what my father thought of this development and made a mental note to ask him as soon as he got home. Clearly the terrorists had set out from Syria and somehow they'd been able to cross the border. Had the security provisions been tightened even further there now? Would he be burdened with even more extra shifts? I just hoped his assignments were not too dangerous. But I also knew that he'd never tell me as much.

Early in the evening Nura and Evin packed their baskets with full jam jars and set off for home. I decided to accompany them and take the opportunity to have a bit of a walk myself. After all, we lived relatively close to one another. Everywhere in the village people had gathered in small groups and were discussing the events of the day. Unsurprisingly, the attacks in the south were the main topic of conversation. But people were talking about what had happened in a strangely detached way, as if it were a natural catastrophe that had taken place in another country altogether. The general thrust was that terrorism was a problem of Shias and Sunnis, who were at war with each other. Nothing like that could ever happen in our neck of the woods. At most, people felt sorry for the Yazidi members of the army, who had to carry the can for the whole affair.

Nura's mother was standing in the doorway to her house with a neighbour. The expression on her face looked serious, but she was delighted by the jam we brought her. 'What a lovely surprise, Farida!' she said, kissing me on the head. 'Is it from the trees in your garden? Please give my thanks to your mother.'

Then she told us that Nura's cousin Ibrahim had contacted his family. Just as we had feared, he had been involved in the fighting in Samarra, and had been shot at too. A bullet had hit his thigh and shattered the bone. Now he was in a military hospital. 'He says it's not so bad and he's being well looked after,' Nura's mother told us. She'd just been speaking with the boy's mother, who naturally was very worried.

'Wouldn't it be better if he came home?' Evin asked.

'They won't let him go,' her neighbour replied sadly. As too many soldiers were looking for opportunities to absent themselves from military service, the army had strict rules, at least for the lowest ranks and for those with no connections to the leadership. 'Let's just hope they really have driven the jihadis from Samarra and that the situation will stay calm there now,' Nura's mother said, ending the conversation.

In Samarra, Baquba and Ramadi it was in fact calm the following day, and the attacks almost seemed like a dreadful nightmare. The jihadis vanished from the face of the earth just as mysteriously as they had appeared. Special forces of the Iraqi army and police secured the three cities. But it would turn out that ISIS had ingeniously distracted the Iraqi military elite from its true target, deliberately diverting our forces.

The next day, 6 June 2014, the first car bomb exploded in Mosul. My younger brothers, who had spent the entire previous day in front of the television, sounded the alarm at once. 'Mama! There's been another explosion!' eleven-year-old Keniwar yelled through the whole house.

My mother and I were just hanging up the washing. We hurried to the television in the sitting room with a mixture of curiosity and foreboding. We would stay there glued to the screen all morning. It wasn't long before there were another four explosions in Mosul. All five explosive devices had been hidden in cars and detonated right next to the checkpoints the army had set up to protect the city from possible attacks. The explosions were a clear statement of ISIS's superiority. 'You've got no defence against us!' they were virtually screaming in our faces.

The poor people of Mosul were screaming too – with pain and worry. The camera showed images of weeping women, shell-shocked inhabitants, emergency medics attending to the injured, and clouds of black smoke above the sites of destruction. They billowed through the busy streets of the metropolis, where chaos appeared to be reigning. Everyone was trying to get to safety. For nobody knew when or where the next detonation would take place.

The newsreader from state television tried to sound calm. 'The injured were taken to nearby hospitals,' said the man from Baghdad with the slicked-back hair and grey-and-white-striped tie. 'There is no reason to panic. Long diversions are in place for traffic. The police and security forces have brought the city of Mosul completely under their control again.'

I didn't like the way he tried to emphasise that everything in Mosul was absolutely fine. Nor how he smiled confidently into the camera. I simply couldn't accept that he believed the words he was reading from his piece of paper. Yesterday Samarra, today Mosul, I thought. And tomorrow? What would happen tomorrow? If the country's second most important city was such an easy target, then probably nowhere in Iraq was really safe any more.

From the corner of my eye I could see that my mother was chewing her bottom lip. She didn't pass any comment on what was happening. But she was quite evidently worried too. Suddenly she got up and went into the garden. Through the window I could see her on the mobile; I suspected she was calling my father. She gesticulated wildly as she spoke to him. Was she perhaps asking him to come home? These were the moments when we missed him dreadfully. But precisely because the situation was so explosive every man was of course urgently needed at the border.

When the car bombs went off on 6 June, we first thought that they were an extension of the series of attacks from two days before. We were shocked by how quickly this metropolis, which was only about one hundred kilometres from our village, had sunk into such chaos. But we had no idea that the situation in Mosul was far more serious. In Samarra, Baquba and Ramadi the terror had lasted for a day, which is why we assumed that it would be similar in Mosul. We were sorely mistaken.

The systematic seizure of Mosul began on 7 June. In the early hours a Kurdish broadcaster reported that a huge convoy of vehicles was heading towards Mosul from the Syrian border, each of these packed full of ISIS fighters. The pickups were transporting hundreds of terrorists and were equipped with mounted machine guns. They overran the blockades on the entry routes into Mosul and drove straight into the city centre. Suicide bombers attacked police and army buildings in a parallel assault. Street fighting ensued. State television ran special programmes all day, which we watched, paralysed.

Mum no longer made any effort to hide her concern from us. 'They're trying to take the whole city!' she said shrilly the next time she spoke to my father on the phone. She even put it on speaker-phone so we could all hear.

'There are 25,000 of my colleagues stationed in Mosul. Do you think they'd let that happen?' Dad's distorted telephone voice clanged from the mobile. 'We've got many times more soldiers than they have, which means the terrorists can't possibly take Mosul.'

'Do you believe that?' I whispered to Delan. He shook his head. Mum gave us a severe look and we shut up.

'The nightmare will be over tomorrow,' Dad promised us from his border post. Behind him we could hear a muffled rumbling. 'I've got to go now,' he said. 'Don't worry and see you soon!'

But he would be proved wrong. The fighting continued. And even though the newsreader tried his best to sound as reassuring as my father, on the second day after the attack it no longer looked as if the army would rapidly get a grip of the situation and drive the terrorists from the city. Soon, on roof after roof, black flags with quotations from the Quran appeared, which the ISIS men had hoisted as a sign of their conquest. The television camera showed us a whole sea of such flags.

The president of Kurdistan, Massoud Barzani, made an offer to the central government to send his troops to defend Mosul. But in Baghdad they clearly still thought they could handle the problem themselves. The government declined the offer with polite expressions of thanks. 'These Arabs are crazy,' Delan groaned. Until recently he, too, had been contemplating a career in the army. But because of the internal tensions in Iraq that had flared up again, he had decided against it. 'They'd rather risk letting Mosul fall into the hands of terrorists than trust a Kurd!'

This decision would come back to roost, and bitterly. On the third day after the onslaught the chiefs of the Iraqi armed forces climbed aboard a helicopter and fled Mosul, a disastrous signal to the forces on the ground. In a panic, the men who were supposed to be defending and protecting the city got rid of their uniforms and weapons, and tried to escape to the south. Those who fell into the hands of ISIS were brutally slaughtered.

In Kocho we were in shock that Mosul had fallen so quickly. One day after the army had so shamefully abandoned the city, the government did give Barzani official permission to defend Mosul with the Peshmerga (the Kurdish militia). But there wasn't anything left to defend. Barzani was able, however, to position his Kurdish fighters further south to defend against future attacks. The government declared its support for this, because it wanted to prevent ISIS from advancing further northwards at any cost. For us, too, it meant that the Sinjar region was now under the protection of the Peshmerga. The Sinjar region is on the edge of Kurdistan, on the border with Arab Iraq. And our village, which lies twenty kilometres south of the mountains, is quite a way into the Arab area. We would far rather be protected by Kurds than Arabs, who historically never proved very loyal to their Kurdish brothers. We'd had quite a lot of quarrels with them in the past. For centuries, Kurds had been suppressed by Arabs, so they were always seeking to gain more independence, and were always ready to defend their homeland, which the government had recently tried to take for Arab oil. After the fall of Saddam Hussein, they have been able to move closer to their dream of being a separate state. As a first step in this direction, they run the militia, the Peshmerga, as an independent army that is not part of the Iraqi forces. That's why our mayor immediately provided a house for the four Peshmerga soldiers who arrived soon afterwards in Kocho.

When my father finally returned from his border duty after these eventful days my brothers and I ran and hugged him furiously. Even my mother, who is usually unsentimental, furtively wiped away a tear, such was her relief at seeing him again, unscathed.

Dad was so ashamed of his colleagues' failure and cowardly flight that he could barely look us in the eye. 'I don't understand it,' he said over and over again. 'They let themselves get seen off by a paltry bunch of terrorists.' In their defence, though, he added that the citizens of Mosul hadn't made it easy for the soldiers. The majority Sunni city had always regarded the army as an alien element, as it followed the orders of the Shia government of al-Maliki, a president they hated and regarded as Tehran's puppet. ISIS had made perfect capital of this.

'Do the people of Mosul prefer the jihadis?' I asked him, nonplussed.

He shrugged. 'These feuds have no logic. Sometimes people need to experience the greater evil to understand which the lesser is.'

Dad went out onto the terrace, sat on a chair and rolled up the sleeves of his uniform, revealing his muscular, suntanned arms. I loved seeing just what a handsome and powerful man he was. As a little child I'd always felt safe and secure in those arms of his. And even now, on the threshold of becoming an adult, I wished for nothing more than to be held tightly by him while somewhere in the distance the world outside was falling apart.

I brought Dad his water pipe that he loved puffing away at in the evenings, and sat beside him. He filled it with his favourite apple-flavoured tobacco. Taking the first drag with relish, he then blew out the sweet smoke.

'I don't want you to go back to the border,' I told him. 'I'd much rather you stayed with us.'

'But, Farida, I have to go back. Who else is going to earn the money so we can all eat? Hmm?'

'But it's too dangerous! These people don't respect any borders. Didn't you see how quickly they got to Mosul?'

'That's precisely why we need men to protect the country,' he argued. 'Brave men. Not cowards who run away when it gets too risky.'

'Who's going to protect us here?' I demanded vehemently.

For a moment Dad appeared to be stumped. But then he recovered. 'You,' he said, giving me a hard stare. 'Or do you think teaching you how to shoot was a waste of time?'

'No, Papa.' I wasn't sure whether he was being serious or joking. At any rate I didn't want to disappoint him.

'You, Delan and Serhad. You're the older ones. You have to look after the rest of the family while I'm away. Do you promise me you will, my daughter?'

I gave a shy nod of the head. He pinched my cheek affectionately. 'Don't be afraid, Farida,' he said. 'They certainly won't get this far. We'll all be on the lookout together: you, me and the Peshmerga.'

Turning his face to the setting sun, he put his hands together solemnly. 'And of course Our Lord. Agreed?'

'Agreed,' I mumbled, partially reassured.

Even the advancing jihadis were powerless against my father's optimism.

But that would soon change.

3

THE CATASTROPHE

I also spent the following days numbed in front of the television, watching what was playing out before my eyes. The terrorists were behaving as if drunk on their success in Mosul. While the inhabitants fled the city in their hordes, they looted banks, museums and government buildings. They freed all the Sunnis who had been imprisoned because of terrorist acts or their affinity to al-Qaeda and made them swear allegiance, thereby doubling the number of their fighters in a trice. It was reported that their next move was to take the capital. Their spokesman, Abu Muhammad al-Adnani, told the cameras, 'Rather than indulging your egos, head for Baghdad.' To the rejoicing of their supporters, his soldiers broke through the earthwork which till then had marked the border between Syria and Iraq. An ISIS man said that the border had been drawn by the 'grandsons of monkeys' and that it was no longer valid. The division of Muslims into separate national states belonged to the past, he said.

The politicians whose speeches I also watched on the television repeated over and over again that the capital was secure. But hadn't they said the same about Mosul? Although the Sunnis were in the minority in Baghdad compared to the Shias, they would doubtless fight on the side of ISIS if it came to a conflict. For this reason some voiced the fear that Baghdad could be overthrown from inside. What would happen next? Would the terrorists conquer the entire country? Thank goodness, I thought, that the ISIS fighters didn't have a foothold in the Kurdish north and the Shia south.

At the beginning of July, a man around forty years old, with close-knit bushy eyebrows and a long grey beard appeared in front of the cameras. This man, wearing a turban and dark preacher's robes, announced that he was the new legitimate ruler of Iraq and Syria. He called himself 'caliph', by which – as I knew from school – he claimed to be both the spiritual and political leader of the Muslims. Not just the Muslims in Iraq and Syria, mind you, but all the Muslims in the world. Such a title, which Abu Bakr al-Baghdadi had selected for himself, implied nothing less than he considered himself to be the successor to the prophet Muhammad.

Of course, state television declined to show scenes of propaganda like this. But a friend of my brother Delan had sent him a YouTube link of the clip, which meant he could view it on his mobile. 'You've got to see this, Farida,' he said. 'This guy founds a new state just like that.' And so together the two of us watched the 'caliph's' inaugural speech.

'Rejoice, await good things and hold your heads high,' al-Baghdadi said in a mosque in Mosul, reminding his followers of how the Muslim world was humiliated during colonial rule. That era has never been forgotten in this region and the sting of indignity continues to be deeply felt. 'For today, thanks to the grace of God, you have a state and caliphate which will restore your dignity and greatness, and win back your rights and sovereignty. A state in which the Persian and the Aryan, the white man and black man, the Easterner and Westerner live together as brothers. A caliphate which unites the Caucasian, the Indian and the Chinese, the Syrian, Iraqi and Yemeni, the Egyptian, Moroccan and American, the French, German and Australian.'

'German and Australian?' I asked Delan, confused. Since when did Muslims live there? What was this man talking about?

'I think he's inviting all the butchers of the world to come to his self-styled Islamic State,' my brother said.

'Or perhaps he means that one day his state's going to be so big that it'll encompass Germany and Australia,' I suggested.

'That's also a possibility.'

'But surely that would mean that he's going to expel all those who don't believe in Islam from these countries?' I continued. Could this really be his plan? The notion that the man in the black robes could be so cruel as well as megalomaniac gave me the creeps. But he had driven out the Christians who'd been living in Mosul for centuries.

My brother put a finger to his lips to shut me up. 'Shh and listen,' he said. 'He's explaining it now.' I pricked up my ears.

'O Muslims everywhere!' al-Baghdadi called out theatrically to his supporters. 'Hurry to your state, yes, *your* state! Hurry, for Syria does not belong to the Syrians and Iraq does not belong to the Iraqis. No, the earth belongs to God alone, who gives it to those of His servants on earth whom He chooses.'

'By which he means himself, I suppose?'

'Who else?' Delan replied sarcastically.

'This state is the state of Muslims,' al-Baghdadi continued, working himself up as his audience kept calling out '*Allahu akbar*' with ever increasing enthusiasm. These people seemed quite pleased with the idea that the world belonged to them. 'O Muslims, wherever you may be, whosoever can emigrate to the Islamic State must do this, for emigration to the house of Islam is your duty.'

'Do you really think that the Muslims will follow him?' I asked anxiously.

'That clown? A self-appointed caliph?' Delan laughed. 'With the best will in the world I can't imagine that the muftis will accept a man like him.'

'Maybe not those in Iraq,' I countered. 'But perhaps he'll find favour with Muslims from other places. I've heard there are many foreigners among his troops.'

'Sure, there are a few loonies all over the world,' Delan said. He winked to cheer me up. Just like my father, he always tried to maintain a sense of humour, no matter how serious the subject we were discussing. I loved this about him. His good mood lent him a very particular charm and in my opinion his fiancée, Zevin, who had recently accepted his suit, had made a good choice. He was bound to be an excellent husband. Any woman would surely be happy at his side.

I felt sorry for the people of Mosul. It must be awful to have a band of thugs attack your city and force everyone living there to live by their rules. It was said that they treated the population with extreme brutality, driving out the Christians and shooting the Shia soldiers one after another. If they wished to avoid being arrested, women had to be fully veiled with a niqab. And anybody who protested was shot or beheaded with a sword. Or at least those were the rumours. What sort of life was that? How could the people tolerate it?

Thank goodness we lived here in such seclusion, at the foot of Mount Sinjar, I thought. Surely nobody would come this far. Because there wasn't anything worth conquering here, no banks, no oilfields, nothing at all. And if someone did try, then there was always the Peshmerga stationed in our village. Officially the Kurdish militia was part of the national army, but it had a particularly good reputation in the north. The soldiers were said to be highly experienced, unswervingly brave and patriotic. They would protect us. Every day the men undertook their patrols to observe the area.

It seemed as if Delan had read my mind. 'Don't worry, sis,' he said. 'The Peshmerga would notice at once if something was not quite right. They'd warn us. And then everyone in the village would take to their weapons – don't forget that every family here has got at least one Kalashnikov. So we'd be able to send those guys running. We'd chase them all the way back to Syria, or wherever they come from. The fact that it's all gone belly up in Mosul is down to those bloody Sunnis – they opened the door to these bandits!'

*

I relied on the word of the two men I trusted most in my life. Both my big brother and my father assured me that I had no reason to worry. The men who had taken Mosul were not interested in us. They'd leave us in peace. In the mornings, when together with my family I turned to the sun, I prayed that Dad and Delan would be proved right.

But then something happened that really scared me. On 1 August 2014, ISIS soldiers attacked a military position in Zumar, a town forty kilometres to the north-west of Mosul, and thus on the edge of the Kurdish autonomous region guarded by the Peshmerga. The town was to the north-east of Kocho. The terrorists also attacked the Mosul Dam and tried to occupy a nearby oil production facility. Fierce battles raged the entire day.

'Those fucking bastards,' cursed my father, who fortunately was not on duty at the time, but at home with us. 'They want to seize the dam. That would allow them to blackmail Mosul and the whole of the south.'

'And the oilfield,' Delan added. 'They were really keen on the oilfields in Syria.'

'What does it all mean?' I asked the two of them anxiously. They exchanged glances, but didn't give me an answer. I knew it myself: the attack meant that ISIS had no intention of stopping at Mosul. It wanted to snare the whole of northern Iraq. Only the Kurds could stop them now. 'Will the Peshmerga be able to deal with them?'

'Of course,' Father and Delan replied in unison – and both of them far too quickly. Once more they exchanged glances that I didn't find reassuring.

All day long we tried to find out what we could about the fighting in the north. For the television news bulletins reported very little and practically none of it was new. Each time the announcers repeated the line that the brave Peshmerga fighters were doing their best against the ISIS forces. My father phoned a number of his colleagues stationed in the area. But they didn't know any details either. And sometimes the rumours they picked up were contradictory. Whereas some believed that the dam had already been lost, others claimed it was securely in Kurdish hands. Some even doubted that it had been attacked at all.

The Peshmerga in our village couldn't help us either. Being simple soldiers they had no information about what was going on in the north. Or at least that's what they said when Delan questioned them. At the end of the day the newsreader on Kurdish television announced that their troops had been victorious: 'The illustrious Peshmerga killed a hundred terrorists,' he read out with satisfaction. But fourteen Kurds had died in the fighting too. 'The patriotic sons of Kurdistan died for our fatherland,' he said.

'That means they defeated them!' I cried out in triumph. 'They sent them packing. That must be what happened!'

'Precisely,' my brother agreed. My father, however, remained sceptical.

'They won this battle,' he said. 'A hundred fighters? Seems a very large number to me. It must have been a huge battle. I wonder how many of them there were to begin with.'

I looked at him. My maths brain went into a spin and suddenly it clicked. Dad was right. If a hundred ISIS soldiers had died today, then the number that had invaded Zumar must have been many, many times larger. After all, the Peshmerga could hardly have managed to kill all the ISIS fighters. Even if that was our greatest wish. So where were the rest of them?

I also thought it suspicious that the newsreader said nothing about the Kurdish war booty. Surely the Peshmerga must have confiscated their enemy's weapons, munitions and vehicles. Where was the footage of the Kurdish military, proudly holding up their trophies to the cameras? The lack of such images could only mean one thing: a significant proportion of ISIS soldiers must have escaped in their military vehicles, together with their equipment. Had they driven back to Mosul? Or had they stayed in the north?

That night I couldn't sleep. A strange sense of disquiet lay over the village. Many people must have been as uneasy as me. It felt like just before a storm: you sensed that something was brewing, that the atmosphere was growing more and more oppressive. But you didn't know exactly what to expect.

At one point I thought I could hear footsteps outside. It was probably the Peshmerga, patrolling the streets, on a high state of alert after the attacks. I wondered whether I ought to go up on the roof and check. I briefly considered taking one of the Kalashnikovs with me, but they were in the chest in my parents' bedroom. So I just climbed up in my nightie.

Then I saw that I wasn't the only one to have had this idea. Among the sacks of cement my father was dozing with his AK-47 in his arms. I tiptoed closer, sat down beside him and nestled up to his shoulder, waking him in the process. 'Farida! Has something happened?' he asked in shock.

'No, Papa. It was just too hot downstairs. That's why I couldn't sleep.'

'Come here,' he said, putting his strong arm around my shoulders. I could feel his heartbeat and breathed in the familiar scent of apple tobacco on his skin. Comforted, I nodded off.

'They've gone!' a voice echoed around the village before sunrise the following morning. Someone was running through the streets crying, 'The Peshmerga have gone! They've left us in the lurch!'

Sleepily I rubbed my eyes, not grasping at first what was happening. But my father sat up with a jolt. 'Is this true?' he called down to the man. 'Maybe they're on patrol somewhere in the area.'

'No, they're miles away!' he called back in fury.

Soon the whole village was astir. My father decided to forgo his morning prayer, hurrying instead to the village square to speak with the other men. Delan and Serhad accompanied him. My mother, my two small brothers and I stayed at home, waiting impatiently for the news they'd bring back. In the meantime Mum switched on the television.

The most important items of news were again about Zumar and the Mosul Dam, the two places where fighting had occurred the day before and during which the Peshmerga had supposedly seen off the ISIS soldiers so illustriously. Overnight, however, they had returned. 'Massoud Barzani now needs every one of his men up there,' my mother said bitterly. 'That's why he ordered the Peshmerga back, leaving us defenceless here.'

When my father and brothers came back they told us that the villagers wanted to form small squads of volunteers to monitor the area. 'It's just a precautionary measure,' Dad emphasised. 'If ISIS people are sighted anywhere nearby it means we can respond in time.'

Mum nodded; it made sense. It was the same job that the Peshmerga ought to be doing. Now the inhabitants of the village were taking it into their own hands. We certainly had enough men and weapons. Dad wanted to set out at once with Serhad and Delan. But my mother objected to this. 'Do me a favour and split up. If something happens I don't want to lose all my men in one go!'

'Nothing's going to happen to us, Zakia,' my father laughed. 'We're just going on a little reconnaissance mission.'

But she was insistent. 'All right. Then Delan can accompany Uncle Adil later on,' my father said finally, giving in.

Mum also insisted that everyone who went carried a weapon. We followed Dad into the bedroom, where he used a key to open the chest that housed the Kalashnikovs. There were still only three of them. He gave one of the AK-47s to Delan, while he and Serhad would take another. 'It wouldn't be a bad idea if you went up to the roof and kept an eye on the street, Farida,' he said. 'Will you do that?' He handed me the third Kalashnikov.

I looked at him, wide-eyed. Father was actually asking me to guard our house. 'No problem,' I said, rather proud of the fact that he had entrusted me with this important task.

The men set off and I went to my post. I weighed the Kalashnikov in my hand. By now I had a pretty good idea how to use it; since my first attempt at shooting with my father, I'd been practising assiduously in the garden. I could even hit the target in the right place: in the middle. But till now shooting had always been a bit of fun for me, like a hobby. Was this now the 'emergency' that Father had talked of? Somehow it didn't feel like it.

I looked at the street, but couldn't see anything unusual. The neighbours were wandering about as they normally would. Perhaps their movements were a little more frantic than on other days. Because obviously everyone was worried. The fact that the Peshmerga had simply disappeared overnight made us all nervous. But then I told myself, of course they've gone! After all, they need to help with the defence of the north, which is in grave danger. Could we resent them for having hurried to help their comrades? Did we imagine here in the south of the Kurdish area that we were more important for the autonomous government than the Kurdish heartland? We had to look after ourselves. With such thoughts and ideas buzzing round my head, I dozed off among the cement sacks as the midday heat approached.

I was woken by the noise of my brothers Keniwar and Shivan playing football around the trees in the garden. And by two women's voices, which drifted up to me from the terrace below. Clearly we had visitors, but from my observation post I hadn't noticed them coming. A fine guard I was turning out to be!

I crawled to the edge of the roof and glanced down. I saw my aunt Hadia, the wife of my uncle Adil, with a toddler on her hip and her two other children. She was a very talented cook, and as a result rather plump in comparison to my petite mother. The two women were having an animated conversation.

'People say that they're in Sinjar,' I heard my aunt say.

'Has Adil seen them?'

'No. But the inhabitants of the neighbouring villages have. There's been fighting, apparently.'

'Are you sure? Sometimes people exaggerate to make themselves sound important.'

'Come on, Zakia, get with it!' my aunt shrieked. 'ISIS is twenty kilometres from Kocho. We're in big danger!'

Finally I understood what they were talking about. There had been an attack on our district capital. 'What happened?' I called from above. The two women turned their heads in my direction and looked up at me.

'Farida!' my mother said in surprise.

'What happened in Sinjar?' I repeated.

'We don't know for sure,' my aunt replied. 'But at any rate . . . they say ISIS soldiers are there.'

My heart almost stopped as she uttered those words. ISIS fighting in Sinjar. That was the worst news that the day could have brought. I left my sentry post and hurried into the sitting room, where I saw my brother Delan who'd arrived together with my aunt.

'They're only rumours so far,' he said.

I switched on the television. But there was only a quiz show on. I couldn't find any reliable information.

My aunt's voice, which we could hear outside, sounded more panicky, however. 'For God's sake, Zakia!' I heard her say. 'Please listen to me. We've got to get away from here. Aziz will say the same when he's back.'

'I just wish he and Serhad would come soon,' my mother replied helplessly.

'They will,' Hadia said, rocking her baby, who had caught the mood of anxiety and now started howling. 'I suggest you get packing. I'm off home.'

They left our property via the garden gate. Mum stood there as if paralysed, as she watched my aunt and her children go. She didn't seem to know what to think or do. Wracked with indecision, she inspected our pantry. It contained rice, beans, eggs, a pail of yogurt, a sack of dried almonds and a few tins of preserves. As if on autopilot, she started packing everything into a large travel bag.

I was just about to return to my post on the roof when she called me: 'Farida!'

'Yes?'

'Tell Delan to relieve you on the roof.' She handed me a shopping bag and a few notes, clearly all the cash we had in the house. 'Go to the shop and buy some food: dried meat, nuts, rice . . . everything you can find. And hurry. Others may well have had the same idea.'

'All right.'

The small shop we usually frequented was one of three in Kocho. When I arrived it was sheer chaos outside. All of a sudden dozens of people had urgently gone shopping. Many of them had come by car. They were carrying entire sacks and crates of food out of the shop, stuffing the boots of their cars with them. I stood at the very back in a queue of about a dozen people.

'That's it. I've got nothing left,' the shop owner said when it was almost my turn. He half closed the shutters. The people outside voiced their protests. But the man had three strong sons who helped him turf out the customers who were still inside the shop and see off all those still trying to get in. I'm not even sure if, in the heat of the moment, he managed to collect the money for all the purchases. All that seemed to matter to him was to close the shop finally and keep what was left of the food for himself.

I hurried to the next shop, which was in another part of Kocho, a fair distance from our house. We would normally go by car if we went there. As every house in the village was surrounded by its own piece of land, Kocho was very elongated.

I'd been striding for a while in the direction of the shop when I heard a pickup stop beside me. 'Hey, Farida!' a very familiar voice cried. It was Nura with her entire family. She was sitting on the rear bed with her mother, grandparents, two aunts and two younger sisters. The men were sitting in the front.

'Where are you going?' I asked.

'Away from here. Isn't your family leaving too?'

'Maybe later. I've got some shopping to do.'

'Spare yourself the walk. The shop near us has closed already.'

'Shall we take you home?' Nura's father offered.

I shook my head. 'I'll try the Ramadis.' That was the third shop.

'OK,' he said. 'But they might be closed too. Don't waste any time!'

Nura leapt down from the rear bed and embraced me. 'Get out of here, Farida,' she urged me insistently. I held her tightly and heard her heart pounding – for the last time. It was unbearable to have to separate like this.

'Look after yourself,' I whispered to her. She nodded.

'And you look after yourself.'

'I promise.'

Then Nura climbed back onto the pickup, and she and her family waved goodbye. I wanted to burst into tears. But I kept my self-control and waved back. 'See you soon,' I called after them, barely believing my own words. When, I wondered, would I see Nura again? Would I ever see her again?

Marching onwards, I discovered that the third shop had its shutters down too, so I returned home empty-handed. Mum's face was etched with disappointment when I entered the house without any shopping. But she was even less pleased when I told her what I'd heard in the village. 'People are driving themselves crazy, even though none of them has ever set eyes on an ISIS fighter.'

When my father finally came through the garden gate with Serhad he was stony-faced: a bad sign. He trudged into the sitting room, the whole family following him uneasily. 'Is it true what the people in the village are saying?' my mother asked, even before he'd taken off his boots. 'Is it true that they've occupied Sinjar?'

My father nodded. 'I fear the rumours are true.'

'We met a man who fled from there,' Serhad said excitedly. 'He says he saw a convoy of armoured vehicles approaching with black flags.'

My mother put her head into her hands.

'The Peshmerga are no better than the Iraqi army. They've left us at the mercy of the enemy,' my father said angrily. 'Two hundred and fifty men were stationed in the Sinjar area. But every single one of them cleared off overnight, making room for the terrorists. Entire villages in the south of the Kurdish area are now encircled by ISIS.'

'That's what the people in the Arab villages are saying,' Serhad added.

'So what are we going to do now?' Mum asked. She pointed to the bag she'd packed with food. 'Hadia and Adil reckon it would be better if we got out of here.'

'Nura and her family have gone too,' I said.

'And where do you think we should flee to?' my father asked.

'To the north, Kurdistan,' I said. I expected that Nura and her family had gone there too.

'How do you imagine we are going to get there?'

I pondered this question. Only one road went through Kocho, so either you could go north, or south to the Arab area, which ISIS had advanced into. That was inadvisable. 'Well, we'll take the road to Sinjar and the mountains,' I said, already realising as I uttered these words that it made no sense because there was fighting in Sinjar as well.

This is exactly what my father was getting at. 'They've got us in a pincer grip. No matter which road we took we'd run straight into the arms of ISIS. It's too dangerous.'

'We met refugees from Sinjar too, who didn't manage to make it to the mountains,' Serhad confirmed. 'They thought they'd be safer here.'

Dad was at a loss. All of us were. What could we do now? All of a sudden ISIS seemed to be everywhere. We were in a trap.

'We have to wait and see how the situation in Sinjar develops,' Dad decided. 'At the moment, at least, it would be suicide to head in that direction.'

Suicide. I couldn't get the word out of my head all that evening and night. My father managed to persuade most of our relatives to refrain from taking the dangerous route for the time being. But no one had warned Nura and her family. They had driven straight into the fighting in Sinjar. I was worried to death about my friend. I kept begging Delan to call her father's phone, as Nura herself didn't have a mobile. But he couldn't get through. 'That doesn't mean anything. ISIS often deactivates the local network when they attack somewhere,' my father said to comfort me. As a soldier he had experience in these things. 'Or he's out of battery.'

My mother, too, tried to reassure me. She was permanently worried that I would get one of my attacks. I'd suffered from epilepsy since I was a small child. Thanks to medical treatment we'd managed to keep the illness under control. But as soon as my emotional balance was unsettled, I developed problems that could manifest themselves as attacks. 'Don't get worked up, Farida. It'll be all right. I'm sure she'll call you in a few days,' my mother said. 'Have you taken your medicine?'

'Yes, don't worry, Mum.'

I went to bed early and fell into a restive sleep, accompanied by bizarre dreams. I saw the man with the black turban and beard, who Delan had shown me on the video clip. The caliph pointed his finger at my friend. 'Nura!' I screamed. Then I heard the rattling sound of machine-gun fire. I sat up with a start. Was I awake or still dreaming? The rattling continued.

I also heard my father's voice, talking animatedly with my mother. The two of them went up to the roof. The night was full of gunfire and shouting. My father was peering through binoculars. 'What's going on?' I asked, still half asleep and yet just as worried as they were.

'Farida, my child.' His voice sounded tender. 'They're attacking Siba.' He passed me the binoculars. 'Look, can you see?'

I could make out rocket fire and explosions in the direction where our neighbouring village lay. Two of my aunts lived there: Rhada and Huda, my mother's sisters. Both of them had small children. My mother tried desperately to get through to them on the mobile. But the network was paralysed.

'I'll drive over to Siba,' my father said. 'We have to help them.'

But Mum wouldn't let him go. 'It's too dangerous,' she protested. 'Their people must be everywhere. At least wait until the sun's up. I don't want to stay here alone with the children.'

He put his arms around my mother to comfort her. And in fact he did wait until dawn. By then the mobile network was working again too, and my aunts called. They had run away from the fighting, fleeing to the hills with the children. 'They've destroyed everything; we've got nothing left,' they said in tears. 'They're shooting at everything: men, women and children.'

'My entire family is dead,' Huda sobbed.

'Where are you now?' Dad asked.

They told him their precise location; it was only a few kilometres from Kocho. 'Come to us straight away,' he said. But they were too scared that Kocho would be ISIS's next target.

'Then I'll come. I'll drive to Siba with a few men.'

'Siba is lost,' they replied. 'You should flee now while you still have the chance. Run for your lives!'

After the phone call my father got through to another relative from Siba, who had also fled. But he only confirmed what my aunts had just said. 'Whatever you do, don't come here,' he implored. 'It's full of ISIS soldiers. The battle is lost. Pack up your things and flee to the mountains, or they'll kill you too.'

My father had heard enough. He informed Uncle Adil and other heads of families in Kocho. All were of the same mind: flight was now the only chance left open to us.

We hectically began packing our things. In the boot of our Opel Omega we stowed, in addition to food, warm blankets, a camping stove, two pots, our three Kalashnikovs and several canisters of drinking water. We also gathered up our valuables: cards, papers, Mum's jewellery, our mobiles. Then we were ready to go, and the seven of us squeezed into the Omega. All the inhabitants of Kocho had done the same as us and were now sitting in their cars. We'd leave Kocho in a convoy heading north and hope we could make it to the mountains. Somehow. 'If you see ISIS soldiers, wave the white flag out of the window,' my father urged us.

Then the convoy got moving. The first cars were already on their way out of the village when the mayor, who was leaving with us, got a phone call. It was from Muhammad Salam, a powerful man in the area. As 'Emir', he was in charge of a number of villages in our region, including the Yazidi villages of Tilbanat, Til Ghazeb, Hatemiyah and Kocho. I'd seen him a few times on one of his sporadic visits. He was a tall, gaunt man with a black goatee, who always wore traditional Arabic robes. He had a pronounced limp as his left leg was lame, and he frightened me.

'Turn round at once!' Salam ordered our mayor. 'You must on no account drive away or you'll pay with your lives. We've come to an agreement with ISIS: if you stay where you are they won't do you any harm.'

'Are there any guarantees for this?'

'You have my word that you'll be safe in Kocho,' Salam said. 'Now, tell all the villagers to turn back. You won't get very far anyway – ISIS soldiers have set up checkpoints on all roads. If you leave, your convoy will come under fire.'

The mayor made a sign for the cars to stop. As I said, some people had already driven off, including Uncle Adil and Auntie Hadia. But most were still in the village. My father and the other men got out and listened to what the mayor had to say. We waited in the car while they discussed the matter with him. Not all the men agreed that you could rely on the Emir's word; many considered him untrustworthy. One made a call to the Yazidi village of Hatemiyah to find out what the situation was there. The villagers said that Salam had also promised them they'd be safe if they stayed.

'All I can do is relay his words to you,' the mayor said. 'Each family must make their own decision.'

From the direction of the main road we could hear gunfire. Clearly the cars that had set off first were being shot at. Some of them turned round to take refuge back in the village. There were bullet holes in the sides of the chassis.

My father returned to us looking gloomy. 'Get out. We're staying here,' he said.

*

ISIS soldiers had formed a ring besieging Kocho. Together with our Arab neighbours they were making sure that no one left the village. Some of the inhabitants tried to slip past the checkpoints at night. Most of them were forced to haul themselves back to the village with bullet wounds. It was impossible to get past the blockades with a large group of people, or even a family.

When we got back home we converted our house into a fortress. My father, mother, two older brothers and I took turns to keep watch on the roof. We always had our Kalashnikovs to hand. And we rearranged the sacks of cement so that they would give us protection should it come to a battle. Now we were expecting an onslaught at any moment. Why otherwise would they bother to encircle Kocho? What did they want from us?

Two days after our abortive attempt to flee, a delegation of Arabs came to the village. These weren't ISIS fighters, but Muslims from the neighbouring villages of Gheravan, Bikatsh and Pisik, around a dozen men in total, including Salam. They drove pickup trucks and instructed all the men to assemble in the village square.

'We've come to an agreement with the soldiers of Islamic State,' Salam explained. 'They won't attack your village. But you have to give up your weapons. That is their condition.'

A murmur of discontent spread through the rows of men. 'Why should we give up our weapons?' the mayor asked. 'We are peaceful people. We only need our weapons to defend our homes and property.'

But Salam was not allowing any dissent. 'We're now going to go from house to house and collect up all the guns,' he announced. 'I advise you strongly to surrender all your weapons. Otherwise our peace settlement is null and void – and Kocho will be attacked in the next twenty-four hours. If anybody hides weapons in his house or refuses to give them up, he'll be endangering the lives of everyone else. The entire village will pay for it.'

Shortly afterwards a couple of Salam's men drove up in their truck. Dad handed over our Kalashnikovs, all three of them. He didn't want to take any risks. 'There's no need to be worried,' the men emphasised as they put them on the rear bed. 'We are Muslims and people of honour; we will keep to our word. You can rely on us.'

'A peace agreement is always better than an attack,' Dad said, probably trying his best to believe it himself. As a soldier, it was a particularly big shock for him now to be standing there without any weapons. It was like a surrender. All the same, we tried to convince ourselves that perhaps this step would ensure the peaceful existence we were so longing for.

Only my mother remained sceptical. 'We have no guarantees. That ISIS lot are capable of anything. Haven't you seen what they're doing to the poor people in Sinjar?'

She was referring to a relative of ours who we'd just heard had lost his life during the fighting in the city, and to the many others who had fled to Mount Sinjar. Iraqi television was reporting that they were stranded up there because everywhere was surrounded by ISIS forces. I imagined their situation to be terrible. I knew from my drives there with Delan that the upper plateau was like a moonscape – no trees to offer shade, no animals and no water to drink. No one could survive up there for long. The people would starve if ISIS didn't let them down at some point. By comparison we had it pretty good here in the village, I thought.

As long as the food lasted, that is. No traders had come into the village since ISIS had surrounded us, the shops remained closed and my mother had already started rationing what we had. But luckily there was the garden too. In summer it provided us with so much fruit that we could have sold some. But of course we didn't; we gave it away to our relatives and neighbours who had stayed behind with us in the village. Evin helped me harvest the courgettes and we gave her two in return. As we sat in the garden we thought of Nura. Neither of us had heard from her since she'd driven off with her entire clan at the beginning of the conflict.

'Do you think they made it?' I asked Evin. 'Do you think Nura's all right?'

'I wish she'd get in touch.'

We were worried about Auntie Hadia and Uncle Adil too. Had their car been one of those shot at by ISIS just outside our village? They hadn't turned round and come back, at any rate. We didn't know whether we should interpret this as a good or a bad sign. Were they and their children now up in the mountains too?

After days of uncertainty my mother finally received a call from Hadia. Her face beamed when she heard her voice. 'We've been so worried,' she said. 'Where are you?'

Hadia said that she, Adil and the children were part of a large group who'd taken refuge near the Solar Springs. It was a place where in good times families used to meet for picnics. Hundreds of cars belonging to Yazidi refugees were already there, she told my mother. For Solar was a dead end; you couldn't get any further by car. Only on foot could you make it up to the plateau, a stony desert without food or water. When they heard that ISIS was hot on their heels, people kept climbing higher. 'Tell Aziz to notify the army,' Hadia said. 'They've got to fetch us from up here.'

'Yes,' Mum replied feebly. She didn't want to discourage Hadia. But this request was asking for far too much. Anybody still able to watch the television news was well aware that neither the Peshmerga nor the Iraqi army was getting to grips with the ISIS advance. By now the terrorists had even taken the strategically important city of Makhmur between Mosul and Kirkuk, and were twenty kilometres outside of Erbil. It was likely that soon they would have conquered the whole of Kurdistan. Given this situation, who was going to be thinking about us or the people in the Sinjar mountains? 'I'll let Aziz know,' she promised Hadia all the same. 'Hang on in there for a bit longer, won't you?'

After the conversation my mother was convinced that our relatives had made a mistake with their hasty escape. 'Look what a terrible situation they're in up there, Farida,' she said. 'We're much better off here at home.'

I thought so too. Until the day when the Arabs came back to Kocho. Just as on their first 'visit', they drove into the village in two pickups and summoned all the men to an assembly. 'What do they want from us now?' my father asked as, obeying the order, he made his way to the village square with Delan and Serhad. Things didn't look good: in contrast to the villagers, who had surrendered all their weapons, every one of the Arabs was armed to the teeth.

Salam's minions helped him up onto the rear bed of one of the pickups so everyone could see him. Then he addressed the men of the village. This time he assumed the almost conciliatory tone of a preacher. 'Today we've come here to invite you to believe in the one true God,' he said and waited for the Yazidis to react. Some shook their heads and whispered to each other. But no one dared protest out loud, as Salam's men were pointing their rifles at them.

'We know that you are devil worshippers,' the Arab continued. 'That is a heinous crime. No one on this earth may pay homage to Satan, or Melek Taus, as you call him. You must renounce this false belief and acknowledge Islam instead. Only thus can your souls be saved.' He spoke a while longer and praised the magnificence of his own faith. 'In our Islamic State we will not tolerate any infidels,' he said finally. 'We will give you three days to make your decision. Otherwise . . .' He gave a menacing pause. 'Otherwise we will deal with you in the way that infidels deserve.'

Salam did not expand on what he meant precisely by this threat. But the men in our village feared the worst. We were well aware of the terrible things that ISIS had done to the Christians in Mosul and the Yazidis from neighbouring villages. People of different faiths had no place in the 'state' of the fanatics.

My father came home utterly crestfallen. He called Mum, my brothers and me into the sitting room and told us what had happened. 'Salam is demanding that we all become Muslims.' He said. 'Every man and every woman in the village must publicly declare their allegiance to Islam. In three days they will come back to hear our decision.'

'In three days!' my mother repeated, as if Dad had just let her know the day on which the world would end. She looked at me, and started to cry. 'Only three more days.'

'Yes,' my father said. Then he told us that he and the other men in the village were agreed that we had to find a way to leave Kocho. Some had already phoned Yazidis in Hatemiyah; ISIS had put the same choice to them, and they were also planning to flee to avoid having to betray their faith.

For one thing was certain: 'We will never deny Our Lord, Melek Taus,' my father said. 'Never! How could we disavow His divine splendour? We are His people, the sons of Adam. It would be better to die.'

'There are things more important than this earthly life,' my mother said, reinforcing his words.

'Our faith is the most important thing of all,' my father reiterated. 'Never forget that. No matter what they do to us. Never forget our fundamental moral laws: respect your elders; never let your heart be consumed by feelings of envy or jealousy; never seek revenge.'

Then we all went outside, turned to face the sun and put our hands together. Dad led our prayer. 'Amen, amen, amen,' he said. 'Blessed be our faith. God will help our faith survive.'

'Amen, amen, amen,' we murmured. I felt the energy of the sun surge through me, and at that moment I was absolutely sure that we'd come to the right decision. As I waited to hear what would happen next, I remembered my conversations with my grandad. He used to a keep an object, a *sanjak*, on the top of his chest of drawers. It was a bronze figure of a bird with a plump lower body. 'Do you know who that is?' he said to me one day.

'Of course,' I replied indignantly. 'That's Melek Taus.' How stupid did my grandfather think I was? I mean, every Yazidi child knew the Peacock Angel.

Grandad nodded contentedly. 'Correct,' he confirmed, bowing slightly towards the peacock. 'As you know, Melek Taus is the most sublime of the Seven Angels of God. He is the most beautiful and perfect of all shining lights. But I'm afraid to say that many Muslims believe him to be the opposite.'

'What?' I asked, as horrified as I was confused. From all the people around me I'd only heard what a wonderful, divine being our Peacock Angel was. And now I was hearing that there were other people who believed the absolute opposite. Where on earth did they get this absurd idea from?

'The whole thing is a misunderstanding,' my grandfather said, 'going back to the beginning of time. When God created the earth and man, He ordered all the angels to kneel before Adam. And what did the angels do?' He raised his eyebrows.

'They followed God's instructions,' I guessed.

'Correct. They did. All apart from one: Melek Taus. He was the only one who *didn't* kneel before Adam.'

'You mean he refused to obey God?' Now I really was astounded.

'Yes, that's right,' Grandad said. 'But he had a good reason for doing so. For the instruction was a test from God. He wanted to check the loyalty of His angels. God wanted to find out whether they actually loved only Him and would refuse to bow down before any other living being. Do you understand now? Melek Taus didn't kneel before Adam, because all his love was for God alone!'

'So he passed the test?'

'Yes. He was the only one of the angels to remain loyal to his Lord. And so God was very pleased with him.

'So what is the problem?'

'The problem is that the Muslims completely misunderstand this story!' the old man said, now worked up. 'They think that God is still raging against Melek Taus. That's why they call him the "fallen angel" and claim he's the embodiment of all evil.'

My eyes were as wide as saucers. 'They think he's the . . . ?'

'Shh!' my grandfather said, putting a finger to his lips. 'You must never utter that name. I'd have to kill you otherwise.' Horrified, I raised my eyes to Grandad to look for the ironic wink in his eyes.

But his expression remained harsh; he wasn't joking. 'Promise me you'll never do that.'

'I promise, Grandad,' I said, pressing my lips together as if to confirm my pledge.

My grandfather started singing softly in his deep bass tones. And I joined in with my young voice: 'O my Lord, you are the Angel, the ruler of the world; O my Lord, you are the Angel, the most munificent king; you are the Angel of the Great Throne; O my Lord you were always the only one from the beginning of all time.'

Finally he smiled. 'Melek Taus is good and merciful, Farida,' he said. 'Never forget that. No matter what others may say about him. And never trust them!'

'Never!' I repeated, clenching my right hand resolutely into a fist. In that moment I understood the extent of our problem: the Muslims regarded us Yazidis as the servants of the Prince of Hell! And because of this tragic misunderstanding they hated us.

Three days later, our mayor informed Salam and his men that we refused to become Muslims. 'After consultation in the village, we've reached the conclusion that we cannot renounce the religion of our forefathers,' he told them. 'We beg for your understanding.'

'Well, then,' the Arabs replied, 'we will notify the ISIS leadership of your decision. We only wanted the best for you.'

'May we hope for mercy?'

'That will be for the caliph to decide.'

'There is no compulsion in religion,' our mayor said, quoting from the second surah of their holy book. But they didn't want to hear this.

'We know what's in the Quran,' they said. 'We know it far better than you do.'

The village of Hatemiyah rejected conversion too. That same night the inhabitants succeeded in slipping past one of the checkpoints. For the Arabs guarding them this was highly embarrassing; they were livid that the Yazidis in Hatemiyah had escaped their grasp. They'd also got wind of the fact that we in Kocho were planning something similar. As a punishment and a precaution, they tightened the ring around our village even further. Kocho was hermetically sealed off on all sides. At every exit from the village stood men from the neighbouring Arab villages, preventing us from planting even one step outside of Kocho. Escape had become impossible.

Our only hope was that the tide of the war would turn decisively, now that the USA was supporting the Peshmerga from the air and bombing ISIS positions for the first time. The mighty power from the other side of the world had also succeeded in creating an escape corridor for those poor people who'd taken refuge in Mount Sinjar and who now had no physical strength left. Together, the Peshmerga and the PKK (the Kurdistan Workers' Party) helped them evacuate.

'You see? There's always hope. We must never lose heart,' my father said. 'I bet they'll come quickly to help us too.'

This hope would prove to be misplaced, however. Whereas we could see from television that our relatives had been finally saved after a week-long ordeal on Mount Sinjar, it seemed as if the world had forgotten Kocho. Although our mayor made many desperate appeals to the government in Baghdad and international aid organisations, nobody came to help us. Perhaps our community of 1,700 souls, which since the start of the conflict had shrunk to 1,300, was simply too small to interest anyone. At any rate, nobody outside took notice of the events looming here.

The thing we most feared came to pass on 15 August 2014. I'll never be able to forget that day for as long as I live. It began like any other August day: with a beautiful sunrise. To honour it in the appropriate way, my family was already up on the roof, performing our morning prayer.

Shortly afterwards it was just me up there. And then I saw them: thirteen vehicles approaching our village. Not the rickety pickups the Arabs had arrived in, but new, white vehicles, mounted with heavy-duty military equipment on their rear beds. In each of them sat ISIS soldiers dressed in black. I had to suppress a scream. In total panic I ran downstairs into the house and informed my father. 'They're coming, they're coming!' I cried. 'They're coming to kill us!'

My mother and younger brothers were immediately caught up in my hysteria and started to cry. 'Is it true?' my mother asked. 'Did you see them?'

'Yes, they're coming from the direction of Mosul. They look just like the men who've attacked all the towns and cities in recent times. But we're no more than a village!'

My father hurried up to the roof, to take a look himself. By now the white vehicles had driven to the centre of our village and positioned themselves at the important crossroads and junctions. 'Yes, those are ISIS soldiers,' Dad said, confirming what I'd seen. 'They've come to loot our properties. They'll take everything we have. It's exactly what they did to the Christians.'

We waited tensely to see what would happen. All of us were terrified. Although my father, Serhad and Delan tried not to show it in front of us, they feared that these could be the last moments we would spend together in our house.

Later that morning the ISIS leaders informed us that all inhabitants of Kocho were to assemble in the school building at midday on the dot. 'Bring all of your valuable possessions,' shouted a group of soldiers roaming the streets and taking the news from house to house. 'Everything of value: cash, gold, jewellery. Your mobile phones. ID papers and credit cards too. Bring it all.'

My father felt he'd been proved right, or at least he behaved as if he did. 'You see?' he said. 'They're thieves. Common thieves. And our Arab neighbours are helping them because they're envious of our possessions.'

'We'll give them everything we have,' my mother said. 'Then they'll leave us in peace, won't they?'

'When there's nothing more for them to steal they'll soon lose interest in us,' Dad promised. But he didn't appear to really believe this. I knew that he was especially worried because he was a soldier in the Iraqi army. Although he wasn't wearing his uniform that day, if ISIS found out somehow it could have terrible consequences for him. He had to be prepared for anything.

'Look after yourselves,' he said. 'And don't forget what I've taught you: faith is the most important thing in our lives.'

'Of course, Dad.'

'Above all, make sure that you finish your schooling,' he urged me and my younger brothers. 'And should anything happen to me, then listen to your mum. I will live on in her.'

My eyes were flooded with tears. 'But what are you talking about, Dad?'

'Nothing. Nothing's going to happen,' he assured me.

We packed up everything we possessed. Our three mobile phones, Mum's gold jewellery, Dad's car keys, our cash and our passports. Then we headed for the school. My father and I out in front, with Delan and Serhad behind us. Mum was holding hands with my two younger brothers at the rear. I can still clearly remember what I was wearing that day: a black blouse and a long, brown skirt. I'd also wrapped a brown scarf around my head. These were clothes of mourning, because so many of our relatives had been killed in Siba and Sinjar. Also, I didn't want the Muslim men to see my face, and given that their own wives veiled themselves, I thought they'd have more respect for me this way.

As we walked to the school, we met many friends, neighbours and relatives. All the women were wearing headscarves. Fear was writ large on everyone's face. Armed men nudged us forward, ensuring that no one took a different path and tried to escape. From a distance we could see the black ISIS flag flying on top of the school building. In the playground more men were waiting for us with Kalashnikovs and machine guns. These were ISIS terrorists dressed in black, as well as Arabs from neighbouring villages, assisting them.

The men demanded that we hand over our valuables. They'd set up a large table to place them on. It was already piled high with all manner of jewellery and cash. 'If you don't give us everything you have we'll kill you,' they warned. They even searched people to check whether they were holding anything back. We were so afraid that we immediately gave them everything.

Then they ordered us to go into the building. It was a strange feeling to enter my school in these circumstances. I had to think of the people I'd normally bump into here: my nice maths teacher, Mr Siamand; the boring physics teacher; and, of course, Nura. Perhaps, it flashed through my mind, my dear friend had done the right thing after all.

They shoved us into the stairwell and instructed the women and children to go up to the first floor. The men were to stay downstairs. I had no idea what that was supposed to mean, but knew I didn't want to be separated from my father and brothers. We didn't even have time to say goodbye. The last thing I saw of Dad was a terribly sad look he gave me as he held hands with Delan and Serhad. I've stored this memory forever in my mind.

My mother, my two younger brothers and I were locked in a classroom upstairs. We stood with the other women and children, densely packed between the window and blackboard, which still displayed a maths problem from the previous term. Everyone was crying and howling. But the terrorists pointed their guns at us and ordered us to be quiet.

When all the villagers had assembled inside the building, I saw Salam limp across the playground. He was wearing the same black outfit as the ISIS people, so he must have been officially one of them now. The only difference was that his beard was quite short. Together with his entourage he entered the school through the main door. We heard him talking loudly with the men downstairs. Later we found out that Salam was again asking them to convert to Islam. First in Arabic, then in Kurdish. I expect he wanted to make sure that they all understood him. 'If you become Muslims, nothing will happen to you,' he promised. 'Anybody who is prepared to change his faith will be allowed to remain in the village. But we'll expel the rest.'

'We've decided no,' our mayor said, replying for everyone. The men muttered their agreement. 'But if you will allow me, I will go and ask the women too. They should be able to decide for themselves.'

His request was granted. Three Arabs escorted the mayor upstairs. His face was as white as a sheet when he stood before us and started to speak. 'Anybody who is prepared to become a Muslim may go now,' he said. 'You may take your children with you. You are free to make up your own minds.'

But all the women stayed where they were. Although we were terrified of what would happen now, a conversion to Islam was not an option for us. I could clearly hear my father's words in my head: death is better than betraying your own religion.

The mayor was taken back downstairs. Shortly afterwards we heard a lorry pull up outside the building. The terrorists herded the men into the playground, barking instructions and keeping them in check with their guns. If anyone tried to run away he was shot at. Out of the window I could see my brother Delan forced to climb into the cargo area with the other men. I had a terrible sense of foreboding. 'What's happening? Where are they taking him?' I asked my mother in desperation. But she couldn't give me an answer.

Soon a second and third lorry arrived, then even some private cars, into which the remaining men were put. I kept my eyes peeled for Dad and Serhad, but I couldn't see them any more. The vehicles drove off in different directions. Panic had broken out among the women in the classroom. 'What's going on? What are you going to do with them?' they kept asking the Arabs.

'We're taking them to the mountains,' they said without any emotion.

But then we heard the shots.

In the distance, about a kilometre away, a cloud of dust flew up.

'You're killing them!' a young woman with an infant on her arm screamed hysterically. 'You're shooting them!'

The armed men just laughed at her. 'Your men are dogs,' one of them said. 'That's why we've got to kill them.'

The women cried in dismay and shock. They threw their heads into their hands. No one could comprehend the utterly pointless cruelty being inflicted on us.

Personally, I was so shocked that I wasn't even capable of shedding tears. My mother, too, stood there numbed and motionless. '*Hazu hu al maktub* – Thus has God willed it,' she said. 'It is our destiny. They're going to kill us too and there's nothing we can do about it.'

4

THE SLAVE MARKET IN RAQQA

In the schoolyard, all the girls around my age stood together in a group. The men had forced us downstairs and out into the playground. They ordered us to split into two groups: all married women with their children on the left, unmarried women on the right. My mother was left standing holding my two little brothers' hands in the other group. I looked at her with sheer horror and she tried to grab me too. But I was wrenched from her grasp by an armed man and shoved over to the group of unmarried women and girls. They aimed their guns at us so no one would get any ideas about running away. I knew all the girls; they were my friends, cousins, schoolmates. Evin was there too. Through the opening in her scarf, which she'd wrapped around her face, she stared at me with her wide-open eyes. In these eyes I could see that she was terribly afraid, as we all were. But of course I could say nothing.

The men ordered us onto a bus. It was a perfectly normal bus like the ones we used to travel around the area. ISIS must have seized the public transport system for its own purposes. I was sure that the moment we were on board it would be the end for us. Which is why at the last second I tried to break away from the group and make a run for it. But an ISIS soldier held me firmly by the arm. 'Do as you're told!'

'I'm not getting in there! Let go of me!' I yelled at him.

'Oh yes you are,' the Arab said, jamming me sharply with the butt of his rifle towards the bus. I kicked out wildly; he became furious.

'Little bitch!' he said. 'We'll soon knock that disobedience out of you.'

He and another man pinned my arms behind my back and dragged me onto the bus, while I screamed blue murder and tried to resist. 'What's the point of all this?' I shouted. 'If you want to kill me, you might as well do it here!'

'We're not planning on killing you, not at all,' the men replied, laughing. 'What a waste that would be!'

They slammed the door behind us and the driver started the engine. He was accompanied by two ISIS soldiers, who kept watch over us during the journey. We girls were absolutely terrified. Some hammered violently against the windows as the bus pulled away. Others were so desperate that they hit their heads against the glass. They'd rather die than look our future in the eye. But no one took any notice of our plight. Nobody could hear us calling for help.

We cried the whole journey. From the road signs I could see that the bus was heading for Mosul. 'Where are they taking us? What are they going to do with us?' Evin sobbed. I couldn't tell her. Although I had a pretty good idea of what was in store for us, I didn't want to say it out loud. In the television reports I'd heard that ISIS was abducting girls from the Sinjar area to give them as wives to its soldiers. Was this really the fate awaiting us too? I found the idea so disturbing that I was unable to take this thought to its logical conclusion. No, it was impossible. Those sorts of things only happened on television, not in real life. There was no way that Evin and I could have got into this situation.

'As soon as they open the door we'll run for it,' I told her.

'But we'll be bang in the middle of ISIS territory.'

'We'll find a way. We have to try.' I sensed that our only opportunity to escape our fate would be the moment the door was opened. This is why I urged Evin to join me.

After a while we reached the outer suburbs of Mosul. It was already dark. We criss-crossed our way through the city, which at first glance didn't look much different from what I'd seen on my previous visits here. This time, however, there were far fewer people in the streets. I saw practically no women, maybe because it was quite late. But there were lots of checkpoints, all flying the black flag. Soldiers kept watch at these, making sure nobody entered the city – or left it – without permission. My heart sank. We really were in the middle of the new ISIS domain. How would we ever escape from this city secured like a fortress?

The bus drove a little further into town, before stopping in a quiet residential street. The door opened. The time had come. 'Right, get out!' the men commanded. Most of the girls hesitated. But I grabbed Evin's hand and rushed outside with her.

A group of armed men was waiting for us. Frantically I looked around for a chance to flee. But realising at once what we had in mind, they blocked our way by forming a sort of cordon. 'In there,' one of them said, shoving us towards the front door of a house, several storeys high and only a few metres away. We had no possibility of going anywhere else.

So we entered the building. It seemed to be a perfectly normal, albeit very large house. The rooms had sofas and chairs, there were carpets on the floors, and even beds and bedclothes. But all of them were jam-packed with girls, every one of them a Yazidi of our age. This was evident from their clothes and the way they were talking. They came from other villages around Mount Sinjar, and I could tell they'd been abducted too, by how distraught they were; some girls were hitting themselves out of sheer desperation.

'Let us go – now!' I shouted at the men. 'We want to go back to Kocho!'

They seemed to find this amusing. 'But we'd far rather keep you ourselves!'

'You have no right! Take us back to our families at once!'

'Your families are dead. We're responsible for you now.'

Hearing this, the girls around me broke into a hysterical sobbing. 'I don't believe a word you say!' I cried. And I really didn't. I thought the men were just trying to intimidate us, to make us compliant. If we lost all hope it would be easier for them to control us.

'Don't listen to them. It's all lies,' I tried to console Evin.

'But what if it isn't? Didn't you hear the shots when we were in the school?'

Of course I'd heard them. 'There's shooting all the time in wars. We don't know what really happened.'

Evin didn't look convinced.

'Look, the Americans are on our side now, aren't they? Perhaps their army is well on the way to liberating us.'

More and more girls from Kocho were being squeezed into the already bursting rooms. Gradually almost all the girls from our school gathered in the house.

At midnight they then started bringing in the really young girls, ten- to twelve-year-olds, who they'd previously allowed to stay with their mothers. Over the course of the evening there must have been a new order from their boss that even the young ones were to be treated as 'women'. After all, the youngest wife of the prophet Muhammad was only nine when they got married.

The young girls were completely shell-shocked. They were still children and had no idea of what was happening. They told us that our mothers and younger siblings had been taken to Tal Afar, a city halfway between Sinjar and Mosul, and in ISIS territory. This was both good and bad news. On the one hand, it meant that our families were still alive; on the other, they – like us – were prisoners of ISIS.

The house was guarded by about twenty men. Half of them stood by the entrance, the rest kept watch inside. A group sat in the hallway, watching television, which was just showing the evening news from Baghdad.

'According to eyewitnesses there has been a massacre in the village of Kocho,' I heard the newsreader say. 'All male villagers are said to have been shot dead.'

The ground gave way beneath me and I sank into a huge black hole. 'No!', I screamed, slapping my face with my hands. Then I started to jerk uncontrollably and involuntarily. I was having one of my attacks. The men turned round and came closer, because they found my behaviour funny. But there was nothing I could do about it.

'Stop that nonsense at once!' I heard them shout from what seemed like far away. But their voices no longer got through to me. No one could get through to me any more. The commotion around me was happening in another world, far away.

I can't properly recollect what I did or didn't do. When I regained consciousness, I was lying on the floor. Evin was bent over me, pressing my arms firmly to the ground. Around me I could see my school friends Rania, Ronahi, Mina and Hanna, looking terrified. They'd never seen me like that before. 'I need my medicine,' I whispered dizzily. 'It's at home.'

Even our guards appeared to be at a loss. 'If you do that again we'll clobber you with a rifle,' they threatened.

It took me a while to come round completely. But then the memory came back to me at full blast.

'Is it true what they said on television? That you've murdered our fathers and brothers? Is it really true?' I said to the ISIS soldiers.

'No, it's rubbish,' replied one of them, who probably just wanted some peace and quiet.

'Don't lie to her!' another said. 'Of course it's true.' This was the same man who'd told us at the beginning that our families were dead. 'You're all alone in this world. You've just got us now. We're your new masters.'

The girls around me started weeping again. 'Why did you do that to them?' they cried. 'Let *us* go, at least!'

'It was our right to kill them because they were infidels. For that is what it says in the Quran: "Kill the Infidels!"'

'And take their wives,' another added. 'That's why you belong to us now, and we can do what we like with you. You don't have any rights.'

'That's a lie!' I snarled furiously. 'You've made it up.' I simply refused to believe that Islam could justify such crimes. 'I know many Muslims who will vouch that it isn't true.'

'But it *is* true,' they insisted. 'Our emir, the caliph, will decide your fate.' I thought of the man with the beard, whose video I'd watched with Delan. At the time we'd made fun of his arrogance. But this man had shattered our lives. Where was my beloved brother now? Was Delan still alive? And Dad? And Serhad? Where had they taken Mum and the two boys?

Evin and I didn't sleep a wink that night. Because there wasn't enough room on the carpets we sat back-to-back, exhausted, our arms around our knees and densely packed in with the other girls. We were only allowed to leave the room to go to the loo. Each time a guard came close we'd give a start, because we didn't know what they had in mind for us next. And of course we were expecting the worst.

Sometime in the morning or around lunchtime they brought us some soup and rice, a portion for each girl. But most didn't touch it. Evin and I, too, refused to accept food from our captors. We just drank a little water. We sat in the room, apathetically, waiting for something to happen.

Then a group of men arrived, bearded and dressed in black like all the others. Heavy weapons swung from their shoulders. A delegation sent by the caliph, apparently. They pranced through the room, ogling us shamelessly. We tried as best we could to hide our faces beneath the veils and scarves we'd brought with us. 'What are you doing?' they barked at us. 'You're not Muslims. Why are you hiding yourselves?'

'Because you're defiling us with your gaze,' the young woman sitting next to Evin muttered. I didn't know her, but she was a particularly beautiful girl. You could see that just by looking into her eyes. Ripping away her scarf, the men were completely dazzled by her beauty. They instructed her to come with them. But the girl stayed where she was, as if rooted to the spot. So they beat her. She started screaming and defending herself with her hands. In the end two men grabbed her by the arms and dragged her out of the room while she kicked wildly and cried for help.

The rest of us sat there as if hypnotised, watching the scene. 'Pigs!' Evin said under her breath.

They picked out a few more, very beautiful girls, interested particularly in the very young ones, it seemed. 'You're very lucky,' they said. 'The caliph has chosen you to be his brides.'

Then it was the turn of the rest of us. A tall, bearded man stood before us, his legs apart. He behaved like a state official. 'Do all of you understand Arabic?' he asked with a strong Baghdad accent. Some of the girls nodded timidly. But most of us didn't react, leaving him none the wiser. 'Your fathers have offended God,' he said. 'They are infidels and they pray to the devil. For this we had to punish them. Death was no better than they deserved.' The girls whimpered softly. 'According to the rules of war and religion you are now our property. We have the right to keep you as slaves. But we've decided to give you a chance. Those of you who are prepared to convert to Islam can become the lawful wives of our fighters.' The man cleared his throat. 'This is a unique chance for you. Renounce your heretical beliefs! Recognise the one true God, Allah! Join our struggle!'

He looked around to gauge the effect of his words. But if he'd been expecting signs of interest or even agreement, he was disappointed. None of us stirred. We just stared at the ground in fear. A few girls who couldn't contain themselves were snivelling quietly. 'Join us, become Muslims!' he exclaimed again. 'Accompany our men in jihad. Become the wives of warriors fighting for a noble cause: a state ruled according to the laws of Islam. A truly pious and just state.'

The only person excited by this appeal was the man himself. He really appeared to believe what he was saying so dramatically.

'If your state is so pious and just, then set us free! Let us go back to our families, where we belong!' I demanded.

He flashed his eyes at me. 'You may visit your families any time you wish. But first you have to acknowledge Islam. For in our state we accept none but Muslims as citizens. If you fail to do this you will not enjoy any civil rights. And we'll treat you like slaves. We'll sell you on the market.'

I looked in horror at Evin. She lowered her eyes and shook her head imperceptibly. 'He's lying,' she whispered. 'Everything he's saying is one big lie.'

'Is this what you want? Anybody willing to accept this fate should stick with her heretical beliefs. The decision is yours alone.' A few girls whispered nervously. Personally, I didn't know what to make of his words. It was as if he were handing us a knife and asking us to plunge it into our own chests. Or those of our families.

'Speak after me,' the ISIS man demanded. '*Ashhadu alla ilaha illallah* – I declare that there is no other God but Allah. *Wa ashhadu anna muhammadar-rasulallah* – I declare that Muhammad is God's messenger.'

None of the girls said anything. We looked at the floor to avoid his furious glare. 'I'm warning you. This is your very last chance!' He recited the profession of faith again. But again we kept staunchly silent.

'Well, you have sealed your fate,' he concluded.

When the man left we anxiously huddled together. 'What do you think they're going to do to us now?' one girl asked apprehensively. 'Maybe we ought to have just pretended to convert to Islam. Just for show, I mean.'

I gave her a look of horror. 'What? So they can marry us off to Muslim killers? The murderers of our fathers and brothers?'

'I'd rather die!' Evin agreed.

'It's true: we'd be defiled forever,' the girl said thoughtfully. 'But perhaps that's how we'll end up anyway.'

'Be quiet!' I hissed at her. 'You must not think like that. Before they lay a finger on us we'll take our own lives.'

We fell silent. Each of us sank into our own, gloomy thoughts. But one thing was clear to us all: if an ISIS fighter decided to make us his wife, our life was over. We would bring disgrace to our families and be cast out of the community. No Yazidi man would want to marry us afterwards. It must not come to that. We bore a responsibility to ourselves and the honour of our families.

Shortly afterwards two buses stopped in front of the house where they were keeping us prisoner. The men shooed us outside, where they formed another cordon to prevent any of us from fleeing.

'Right, then! We're going on another trip,' they said.

'Where are you taking us?'

'You'll see.'

When I saw the buses I couldn't help thinking of how I'd watched our men being loaded onto the lorries. I stayed planted to the spot and made no move to follow the instructions. 'If you refuse to tell me, I'm not going anywhere,' I announced.

'Oh yes you are,' one of the armed men said, hitting me with his rifle.

'We're taking you back to your parents,' one of his colleagues said.

'Is that true?' Evin asked.

'Yes, to your mothers in Tal Afar.' He laughed.

'He's talking nonsense. We're taking you to Syria,' said the first man. 'We're going to sell you at the market.' He laughed, too, making it impossible to know who was telling the truth. Neither of them, probably. We started to panic. Some of the girls tried to run back inside the house. The one thing they didn't want was to go even further away from home.

'That's enough talking!' another man yelled. 'Get in!'

They violently shoved us into the vehicles. I held on tight to Evin's hand so at least we'd get on the same bus. For me that was some consolation. Whatever they had in store for us, at least my friend would be with me. At that very moment, this was the most important thing.

We set off westwards in convoy, towards the setting sun and our homeland. One car drove in front, another behind. Three ISIS soldiers, young men around twenty years of age, had been detailed as guards; they travelled in the rear of the bus and kept their eyes on us. I didn't let go of Evin's hand for a second.

First we came to Tal Afar, the place they had allegedly carted our mothers off to. We were all gripped by a nervous hope. Perhaps the man hadn't been lying after all. Perhaps we would see our families again. But rather than stop, the bus kept going towards Sinjar.

Soon we were at the foot of the mountain range where so many of our relatives had fled. Had our families now been banished there too? Maybe the men were going to drop us off up there. There was nothing we wanted more keenly! Even the wilderness of these mountains seemed preferable to remaining under the control of these barbarians.

When we realised that the bus wasn't going to stop there either, there was renewed agitation among us girls. 'Stop!' some cried. 'Let us out!' But I knew that they wouldn't let us go voluntarily. So I tried smashing the window with my hand. I slammed it with all my strength, causing a loud noise that our guards heard too. But the window remained intact, and my hand hurt terribly.

The guards became angry, of course, when they found out what I'd been trying to do. One came up and hit me hard in the face. Then he sat between Evin and me so that we couldn't attempt any more escapes. He tried his very best not to touch either of us. But now other girls were also trying to smash the windows. 'Let us out!' they screamed. 'Let us die here, in our homeland!'

The ISIS men were totally on edge. The young man who'd been sitting between me and Evin stood up and walked to the front of the bus. He turned and aimed his rifle at us. 'If you don't shut up at once I'll shoot the lot of you,' he threatened.

We fell silent.

The bus kept going westwards towards the border that my father had been guarding until recently: the border between Iraq and Syria. But it no longer existed; all the border posts had been bulldozed. Our bus continued on its way without any controls. The 'Islamic State', as our abductors called the entity they had created, now extended across large parts of northern Iraq and northern Syria. Just as the caliph had predicted in his address in Mosul, the territory was now indeed the size of a state, larger than several others in the region. How, I asked myself, had this come about in such a short period of time? Only two months ago most of the people in our village hadn't even been aware that there was a terrorist group called ISIS.

We kept driving through the night. And although we were dead tired, we couldn't get any rest. I spent the whole time staring out of the window, looking for signs with place names. We were desperate to know where we were. At one point I saw that we were approaching the city of Raqqa. This metropolis in northern Syria was the de facto capital of the 'Islamic State'. Was it also the destination of our journey?

After almost ten hours in the bus we stopped outside a low, elongated building. It stood behind a wall of earth topped with barbed wire. The building was guarded by a group of ISIS soldiers. They sat with pistols and machine guns in front of the entrance, a sliding metal door secured with several chains. 'Fresh supplies! Lovely young Yazidis!' one of them joked. Together with our guards they took us one by one from the bus and into the building. When we were all in, they slammed the door shut behind us and secured it again with the chains.

We were inside a large, brightly lit hall. Eighty girls were already there, and they all seemed to be Yazidis. Some had been lying asleep on the ground. When we entered with the men they covered their faces with veils. But we could still see their puffy, tear-stained eyes. Their clothes smelled as if they hadn't been changed in a while.

I recognised a young woman I'd once met on one of our pilgrimages to Lalish. With her moonlike face and oval eyes she was a real beauty. Her family had camped near mine. But all that seemed to belong to another era. She recognised me too. 'You're from Kocho, aren't you?' she said, looking at the girls who'd arrived with me.

'That's right. What about you?'

She said the name of a village at the foot of Mount Sinjar. 'They captured us as we were trying to flee to the mountains,' she said. 'We thought Kocho had been spared.'

'No. It looked like it might be to begin with. We were given a guarantee of our safety. But two days ago the Arabs attacked us.'

'We were abducted a week ago.'

'What goes on here?'

'This is a . . . prison,' the girl said, faltering. I had a keen sense that she wasn't telling us everything. 'But it's not a permanent prison. They keep coming to take girls away.'

'Who takes them away? And where to?'

'The ISIS men. They come every day.'

'They're selling us,' another girl said, uttering those words that the first one hadn't been able to.

I felt giddy. When they heard this the girls who had arrived with me started crying again. In their desperation some tried to run to the door. So the self-styled caliph's announcement in Mosul that he'd be selling hadn't been an empty threat. The slave market he'd talked about was here in this very hall.

Evin was worried about me having another attack. She helped me sit on the floor and fanned air in my face. 'How could they do this to us? Who gives them the right?'

'These aren't people, they're monsters,' she said. 'But they'll get their comeuppance one day.'

Evin put her arm around me, stroked my hair and whispered words of comfort. She calmed me as a mother does a child in distress. At that moment I realised that she was the only close friend I still had. Apart from Evin, nothing of my old life remained. I sensed that I'd die if she were taken from me too. 'Promise you'll stay with me,' I said to her.

Evin gave me her word. 'I'll look after you,' she said.

Our prison was essentially the hall we spent most of our time in. Besides this, there was a back room with empty shelves, a sitting room-cum-office, with carpets and sofas, a rather dilapidated bathroom with a washbasin and loo, and a small inner courtyard, completely surrounded by high walls and barbed wire. The only window was in the sitting room, and it was secured with metal bars. Through it you could see the Euphrates flowing past. We reckoned that the building had previously been used as a warehouse. Perhaps industrial goods had been stored, bought and shipped here. Perhaps ISIS had driven out the owner. Or he'd already left the place to flee the civil war. We didn't know. All we did know was that now *we* were the goods the men were selling. It soon became clear that this building on the edge of Raqqa was the main warehouse and market for kidnapped Yazidi girls.

The morning after our arrival the guards brought us cheese sandwiches and water. We were too starving, too dehydrated and too weak to reject food again. Greedily we quenched our thirst and devoured the sandwiches. For such is the human body: in the end it wants to survive and so forgets its pride.

Then the first customers arrived. From a distance we could hear the engines of cars approaching and parking by the earthwork. The girls who'd been prisoners for longer immediately wrapped their scarves around their faces. Evin and I followed their example. By the entrance outside we could hear our captors greeting the other men. They took off the chains, unlocked the door and let them in: a large group of ISIS fighters in dark garb. Many of them had long hair and beards, some wore turbans. All of them were carrying heavy weapons and were quite clearly in a good mood. 'So we have a nice lot of new arrivals, do we?' one of them asked.

'Forty-seven young Yazidis arrived only last night,' the highest ranking of our guards confirmed in his Palestinian accent.

The customer looked around with keen interest. 'And which ones are those?'

'All you new ones, stand together in a group!' our guard ordered.

We ignored his command. A few girls turned to face the wall. Others tried to escape into the rooms at the back. It was a hopeless act of resistance, as the men with their rifles barely allowed us to move a centimetre.

'Enough shenanigans,' the Palestinian said, calling us to order. 'You're now going to line up like good girls. Hurry up!'

His helpers dragged us to the middle of the room and tore the scarves from our faces. We resisted and screamed. But they beat us with such brutality that we shut up. Terrified, we stayed where the men had put us. 'Lift up your beautiful little heads,' the Palestinian ordered, running his finger under the chin of one of the other girls to make her raise it even further. 'And now show me your hands,' he demanded. Trembling, she stretched out her arms towards him and turned her palms upwards, making it resemble slightly our stance when we pray. The sight of her made me particularly sad.

'Yes, very good,' he said. 'Now the rest of you – stand like this too! After all, we want to get a proper look at you, don't we?'

None of us offered any further resistance. The men walked along the rows, giving the girls a thorough inspection, one after another. They chatted in a variety of dialects; I detected the familiar Arabic of Iraq and Syria, but also the Egyptian and Tunisian vernaculars I'd only heard on television before. I thought I could identify another man, who had a long, especially thin beard, as a Saudi by the way he spoke. They were an international bunch, but I understood them all. 'They're hot, these Yazidi girls,' I heard one say close to me.

'Are all of these girls really still virgins?' another asked.

'They're unmarried. Nobody has touched them,' our Palestinian guard assured the men. 'As I said: fresh goods.'

The interested parties nodded their satisfaction. 'We'd have to try them out to be sure,' one said. This same man, a rather portly individual with chubby cheeks and a sparse beard, suddenly stopped beside me and gave me a stare. I felt ashamed and tried to hide my face behind my long hair. But he stroked it away with his sausage-like fingers and kept ogling me. His gaze was brazen and lecherous.

'Hey, you,' he said. 'I particularly like the look of you. How old are you?'

I didn't reply.

'Come on, tell me. You do understand me, don't you?'

I stood there as stiff as a statue, saying nothing.

'Does she understand Arabic?' he asked, turning to the men who guarded us. But they were clueless.

'They talk Kurdish to each other, but some can speak Arabic too,' they replied vaguely. The man nodded. I watched him stretch his arm out towards me again. His fingers touched my lips. When he tried to push my jaws apart my heart started thumping like mad. It seemed as if he wanted to check the quality of my teeth. I was reminded of the livestock market in Kocho; this is how the men would check donkeys and cows before buying them. 'Quite meticulous, aren't you?' his friends quipped.

Instinctively, and out of the blue, I bit him as hard as I could. The man yelped and pulled his hand away. The sausage finger was bleeding. 'You bitch!' he cried. 'You bit me!'

His mates made fun of him, but he became absolutely livid.

'You won't do that a second time, my girl!' he shouted, violently ramming the butt of his rifle into my stomach. I bent double with pain. He kept thrashing me, then I fainted. The last thing I recalled was that familiar feeling of giddiness.

'Watch out! She's falling,' I heard one of the men say. But it was too late; I began to jerk and my face twisted into grimaces. I'd lost control over my own body in another of my epilepsy attacks. Before the eyes of everyone else my body performed contortions I wasn't aware of myself. For me the world outside had ceased to exist. My consciousness had turned inwards. 'She's ill.' Evin's voice came to me from the distance. 'Can't you see she's ill?'

When I came round I was lying on one of the sofas in the sitting room. A girl was fanning my face. And Evin was still talking to the man who had beaten me. 'Farida is ill,' she reiterated. 'She needs medical attention. If you take her you have to be aware of this.'

But the man had seen enough for the time being and had lost interest in me. The group took fifteen girls from Kocho altogether;

Evin and I were not among them. But we could hear the screams of our friends as they bound their hands and took the girls outside to load them into their cars.

There was no closing time at the slave market in Raqqa. The sales display was open round the clock. Men came into the hall at any time of the day or night to inspect the wares.

Some were seeking a slave for themselves. If they'd come to Syria from abroad their wives were often too far away to look after them. Which meant they wanted a replacement for the duration of their time away. The Syrians, on the other hand, often already had a wife with them, but were looking for one or two more to help out at home. Then it was particularly important that the girls in question spoke Arabic, because they would have to understand instructions and be able to communicate.

Other men were sent by their bosses, who wanted some fun but didn't have any time to do the shopping themselves. Or they were after a 'present' for someone they owed a favour. And slave girls were also in great demand as barter goods. In such cases the buyers were especially after young and dainty girls who would please the other man and not cause any trouble. After all, they didn't want to risk any 'complaints'.

The men voiced their wishes and preferences candidly. In conversation they'd frequently reassure each other that they were justified in enslaving us because, as non-Muslims, we were not their equals as people. As pious Muslims they were the master race and we were subhuman. And in a group where everyone thought the same way, perhaps after a while they actually believed this to be true. We, however, made every effort to upset their view of the world. 'What you're doing is wrong,' we told them. 'Your religion does not allow you to kidnap and sell women.'

'Only Muslim women enjoy our protection,' they'd reply. 'Infidels like you have no rights at all.'

'But we're married!' we claimed. 'And in your faith it is a sin to use another man's wife.'

'You're lying,' our guards said. They hated it when we said such things because it had a bad effect on the price. 'All the girls here are unmarried.'

'What does it matter?' one of the ISIS men said. 'If their husbands are dead we have the right to take them for ourselves.'

The others expressed their agreement. Some even spoke of a fatwa supposedly permitting such behaviour. In reality, however, they must all have been aware they were committing a crime, because neither Islam nor any other religion in the world endorsed the trade in abducted women.

Only once did we see the mask slip from one of the men. He was a Syrian and came with his friend or colleague from a local ISIS unit in Raqqa. As usual we had to line up before them and stand upright, so they could see and examine us from all sides. The man's friend picked out a girl, then retired to the sitting room with our captors to negotiate a price, while we remained in the hall with the other man. We were still standing there rigidly, waiting for him to decide too. But he just stared at us sadly, making no move to come closer.

'You poor creatures,' we heard him say all of a sudden, when he was sure that nobody apart from us could hear him. 'If it were up to me I'd let the lot of you go. I'm really sorry that you have to put up with all this.'

We thought at first that we'd misunderstood him. Evin, who was standing beside me, was the first to grasp what he'd actually said. Falling on her knees before him, she begged, 'Please, good man, take us with you. Me and my sister. She's ill. She needs help.'

I kneeled before him too. 'Please save us!' I implored him. 'We'll serve in your house.'

But the man shook his head. 'I can't,' he said, embarrassed. 'I can't take you with me. My family would never accept it. They'd pour scorn on me if I brought two Yazidi girls home.'

'Then take Farida with you at least! Take her as a servant girl,' Evin begged. 'She's a good cook and will be of great help to your wife.' But he merely shook his head again.

When his friend came back the man didn't say any more. Of course, it would have been too dangerous to express his opinion in front of the others. We understood that. And yet we were deeply disappointed when he left the hall without taking any of us with him. Thus vanished our potential saviour. He was the only one of the men who I saw with anything approaching a conscience. But he wasn't going to risk anything for us Yazidi girls.

Our group shrank. Every day new men arrived to buy girls and take them away. I can't remember how many times we had to line up and let them ogle us. For us, time became blurred. As we had nothing to change into, we still wore the clothes we'd had on when our village was attacked. I spent the whole time there in my black blouse and brown skirt. Evin was dressed entirely in black. We barely washed either, even though, as I said, there was a basin. Why should we bother? We didn't want to smell or look nice, but appear as unattractive as possible.

Of all our captors, we hated the Egyptian and Palestinian the most. They kept coming out with obscene comments. The Syrians were slightly better mannered, which may have been down to the fact that they weren't hardened ISIS fighters, but only nominal members. They'd joined the group opportunistically when ISIS conquered northern Syria. But they, too, didn't hesitate to abuse their new power over us. The opportunity to acquire us as 'slaves' was an enticing option to them.

Whenever we noticed that a man was interested in us we would try to put him off. The moment someone touched me I would immediately start screaming and hitting myself. They needed to know straight away that I would not fulfil their desires. Evin, who always stood beside me, but was in less demand because of her age, warned them that I was ill. This was no mere ploy; because I couldn't take my medicine I did have a number of bad attacks during this period. And each time I'd be harshly beaten for it. But over time my captors came to realise that I couldn't do anything about it and that I urgently needed medical assistance. 'Tell the men that Farida's your sister,' one of them advised Evin. 'Maybe then you'll both get taken together.'

Essentially, of course, we didn't want to become the 'possession' of any of these criminals, either together or separated. But the fewer girls there were, the more dangerous our situation became. At the presentations the choice became ever smaller. We knew that we wouldn't be able to put off our sale for much longer. So I said to Evin, 'We've got to get out of here. We must find a way to escape.'

With the other girls that remained we debated whether we could overpower the guards at the door. They already suspected that we were hatching something and they tried to scare us. 'If any one of you tries to escape we'll shoot you on the spot,' they warned us.

'But we've got to try,' I whispered. 'The next time they open the door for customers we'll rush them and grab their weapons.'

Evin and the others gave me a look of horror. 'How's that going to work? Only two of us can get through the door at a time,' they objected. 'That's not enough to deal with those guys out there.'

They're right, my maths brain told me. As soon as the first girls were out they'd be nabbed by the men before anyone else had left the hall, and the door would be shut again. It couldn't work. Feverishly I thought about what else we could do. Wasn't there another way out? We searched the entire building for an alternative escape route. But the only window was secured with those strong bars and the walls in the courtyard were too high to scale. Nothing. Then chance came to our aid. Evin came rushing into the hall from the back room, looking unusually happy. 'I've found something!' she announced.

'What?' we asked, full of curiosity.

'This!' Triumphantly she held out a pair of pliers.

'That's unbelievable! Where did you get them?'

'They were in a cardboard box behind one of the bookshelves.' Someone must have left them there and forgotten about them.

Now our situation looked quite different. With pliers we could try to break the locks on the door when our guards were sleeping at night. But what if one of them woke up? Then they'd give us short shrift. It was an undertaking fraught with danger. I deliberated again and came up with a better idea: we'd use the pliers to get rid of the bars by the window on the other side of the building. Then we could all escape together at night across the Euphrates.

It was a brilliant plan. The very thought that it might work lifted our spirits. As soon as we sensed we weren't being watched Evin and I got down to work on the bars with the pliers. To begin with we tried to cut through them. But they were too thick. So we resorted to bending them to the side, to create a space we could squeeze through. But that, too, was harder than we'd thought. The metal turned out to be incredibly unpliable and robust. Evin cast me a look of dismay. Would our physical strength ultimately prove insufficient to overcome the material?

'Come on, keep going,' I encouraged her. 'We can't give up. We simply have to do it.'

We took turns. Meanwhile the other girls kept an eye on the door to the hall, so they could warn us in time if our guards approached. We had bent the bars quite a way when the alarm was suddenly raised. A girl came running to us. 'Stop right now!' she said. 'They're coming!'

We hurriedly hid the pliers beneath my skirt and went over to the others. The chains were rattling and the metal door was being slid open. Our captors led two men into the hall. I will never forget the sight of them.

One was an ISIS fighter from Libya. Tall and thin, he looked mean. He had a long beard and long, bedraggled hair, as was the ISIS fashion. I heard him referred to as Abu Afram. From the outset he repulsed me. The second man, a rather pale and chubby guy, was called Eleas. He was an Iraqi from Mosul and looked nothing like your classic ISIS soldier as he was clean-shaven with short hair. In spite of this the two men acted like friends or colleagues, although the Libyan called all the shots.

They stalked along the rows which, as I've said, had thinned out quite considerably; only about forty of us were left now. The men stopped in front of a few girls. Abu Afram touched their faces and legs, to 'check the quality', as he put it. He took a particular shine to Amna and Lena, two skinny teenagers with fearful eyes and long brown hair. Lena had remarkably white skin, which is considered very beautiful in our region. They were too shy and frightened to utter a word. I became nervous. If we were going to attempt an escape tonight we wanted to take our friends with us. These men must not whisk them away beforehand.

'Each one more beautiful than the next,' he said to the Iraqi. 'How can one possibly decide, Eleas?'

'Why not take a few of them if the choice is so hard?' our captors said.

I looked at the greed on the men's faces; they seemed to like the suggestion. 'Not a bad idea. Several girls would certainly mean more fun.'

The Iraqi nodded in agreement. 'But we ought to talk about the price again.'

'Of course we'd give you a discount in that case,' our captors assured them.

They withdrew to the sitting room to discuss the matter. I exchanged anxious glances with Evin. If they weren't completely blind they'd notice now that we'd warped the bars. My heart began racing. Was there any possible way we could prevent this? No, there wasn't.

We didn't have to wait long before the chief of our guards, the Palestinian, came striding back into the hall. 'Who did it?' he asked us in a fury. We looked at him simple-mindedly, acting as if we didn't have a clue what he was on about. 'Which of you tried to break the bars in there?'

No one said a word.

'If that girl doesn't own up I'm going to punish you all,' said the Palestinian. 'Come on!'

We stood there with ashen faces, but remained silent. He fixed his stare on us. 'I *will* find out who did this,' he said menacingly. 'And when I do, woe betide . . .'

His gaze slid across our faces. I was terrified I might give myself away somehow. So I looked at the floor. But that was exactly the wrong reaction. Seeing as I always made such a scene when anyone came too close to me, he found this strange. He examined me more closely and discovered the bump beneath my skirt. Shamelessly he felt my hips and then proudly pulled the pliers from the waistband.

'Well, well, well, if it isn't our crazy little girl,' he said. 'Up to your stupid tricks again. As if we didn't have enough trouble with you already.' He gave me a resounding slap. My head droned and I had difficulty staying on my feet.

Then I saw the Libyan approach me. 'So she tried to escape, did she? How sweet!' he said. 'She seems to be full of beans, this one.'

'She's the bride of the devil,' the Palestinian said in irritation.

The Libyan looked at me with growing interest. 'How much do you want for her?'

'I'll make you a special price if you get her out of my sight.'

'Hey, little one,' he said, turning to me. 'Do you speak Arabic?'

'No, she doesn't understand a word,' Evin answered for me. 'She's my sister and she's ill.'

He was undeterred. 'We can only go together, because I have to look after her,' I heard my friend say. I was totally overwhelmed by her self-sacrifice. My friend was really willing to give herself up to this barbarian to protect me! At the same time I was engulfed by a profound sadness. If only the men had turned up to our prison a few hours later, the other girls and I would have been long gone.

'All right then, you can come too!' Abu Afram laughed. He was delighted at the prospect of even more slaves for even less money.

He seemed entranced by the idea of taking a whole sackful of girls home.

Our captors just wanted to be rid of us. They'd had enough of Evin, and especially of me, the persistent troublemaker who scared away customers with her attacks. So they were very keen to make a deal. Abu Afram took Evin and me; his Iraqi colleague, Eleas, took Lena and Amna. He was going to have them picked up later.

I'd have liked to know how much we cost. But I never found out.

5

IN THE DARK ROOM

Sold. It took me a while to realise what had just happened: I'd been traded like an animal at the livestock market. The men who'd kidnapped and kept me captive had peddled me. They'd earned money by relinquishing me to other men who could now do with me as they pleased. Who regarded me as their property, as their 'slave'. And all those involved behaved as if their dealings were perfectly legitimate and normal. How could these people justify their deeds before their God? Did they seriously believe, as they kept insisting, that He gave them the right to do this? Would He forgive them? I, at any rate, would never be willing to do so.

I screamed and kicked when they tied my hands and put me in a black full-length cloak, which now was obligatory for women in the ISIS realm. As much as I'd wished to leave the hall over the past few days, at that moment I was terrified of doing so, terrified of what would happen now.

I glanced at Evin. Her face was pale too, but she looked as composed as ever. Blinded by the dazzling sunlight of that August afternoon, we screwed up our eyes as they shoved us out the door. After spending almost ten days in the prison, we were no longer used to the rays of the sun, our beloved and venerated sun. We almost felt as if it had deserted us. But there it was. I bent forward imperceptibly and offered a hurried prayer to the heavens. 'Lord, please let everything turn out all right. Let us find a way to escape them,' I whispered silently.

We walked past the guards with their American M16 machine guns and Russian Kalashnikovs. The same men who'd brought us our cheese sandwiches in the mornings. And sometimes a plate of rice too. They'd threatened to shoot us if we tried to escape. And we'd believed them. But now it struck me that all their threats had been hollow. They'd never have shot us. We were far too precious as goods for that. But fear had prevented us from realising this.

They grinned as we passed them on our way outside. I really wanted to punch them in the face. Why had I let them intimidate me? I'd rather have risked being shot. Then at least I'd now be free – or dead. And that would definitely be preferable to being carted off by these vile criminals. With Abu Afram and Eleas at either side of us, we squeezed our way through a gap in the barbed wire that was coiled on top of the sandbags, and went down to the cars. Among the military vehicles there was a smaller four-by-four. The men ordered us to get in the back. Reluctantly, we obeyed. At once I started to scan the vehicle for potential ways to escape. Was there a child lock on the doors?

'Do you think we might be able to jump out while the car's moving?' I whispered to Evin in Kurdish. At that moment I heard the 'click' of the central locking. With that, my plan was ruled out; we were trapped in the car.

'Hey, we only speak Arabic here!' the men bellowed from the front.

'My sister doesn't understand Arabic,' Evin reminded them.

'Then tell her to keep her trap shut!'

We drove every which way through the city. I was surprised by just how much activity there was in the streets of Raqqa. I'd always imagined this capital of terror to be a bleak place, with only sinister figures about. Men like the ones who'd kidnapped and kept us captive. Men like the one who'd bought us and was driving this car. I'd heard of the executions carried out here in broad daylight, of the expulsions.

But looking out of the window now, I could see or sense nothing of the horror that had taken place here.

There were many small shops and kiosks still selling food, snacks and other items: cosmetics, electrical goods, furniture, clothes. You could even buy football shirts here, in spite of the ISIS occupation. It was only the plethora of black flags flying from the rooftops that made it clear who was in power here. All billboard advertisements had been pasted over with ISIS propaganda posters. Virtually every male inhabitant of the city now wore a beard, or at least stubble. And all you could see of the few women venturing out into the street was a mass of black material. They were completely covered, even their eyes.

But otherwise everything looked quite 'normal'. After murder life goes on, evidently, I thought bitterly, and in my mind's eye I saw my own village. Was Kocho now inhabited by Muslims? Were black flags flying on rooftops there too, and fully veiled women scurrying through the streets? Perhaps the women from the neighbouring Muslim villages? I couldn't really imagine it. But it wasn't impossible. For certain the conquerors had helped themselves to our property.

We stopped at one of the kiosks by the side of the road. The two men got out, locked the doors and bought crisps, chocolate bars and bottles of water and orange juice. The vendor, a man in civilian clothing, peered nosily into our car as he attended to their wishes. I briefly considered screaming to alert him to our predicament. But the obsequiousness he displayed towards Abu Afram stopped me. The Libyan who'd bought us was clearly an important ISIS figure. No civilian would dare risk a conflict with him just to help us out.

So on we drove, out of the lively city centre and into a district called Rabia, as I saw on a sign. The road leading there was unsurfaced and full of potholes. The district itself looked desolate too; ruins and rubble were all that remained of many houses. The Assad government must have attacked this part of the city from the air and most inhabitants had taken flight.

We finally stopped outside a house with a number of apartments. Half of the building was missing; it must have been torn apart by a bomb too. The remaining apartments on the other side were blackened with soot. Some windows were also missing. Evin and I looked at each other in apprehension. 'Where are you taking us?' my friend asked the men.

'We're going to stay the night here,' they replied. They let us out and took us up to the third floor, where in fact there was a perfectly normal locked door.

'Do you live here?' Evin asked.

'Yes,' they said. The Iraqi unlocked the door and led us into an unbelievably filthy apartment on two floors. The entire floor and even the stairs were covered in a fine layer of soot. Otherwise it was practically empty: only a few chairs, what was left of a kitchen and a heap of rubbish.

'What *is* this?' Evin asked again. 'What are we doing here?' With the best will in the world we couldn't imagine that this wrecked hovel was the men's home. It must be an apartment occupied after the original owners had fled the fighting.

'It's just a stopover,' the men declared. 'Tomorrow we'll take you back to your families.'

Evin and I looked at each other, knowing that they were lying. What did they really plan to do with us? Were they traffickers in women, who were going to sell us on? Or were they going to set up a love nest here?

They put us in one of the rooms. 'Wait here, we'll be right back,' they said, locking the door from the outside. We heard them go down the stairs and drive off in the car.

'What is this all about?' I asked Evin.

'I don't know. But we can't expect anything good to come of it, that's for sure. Either they'll sell us or they want us for themselves.' She looked at me sadly. I knew exactly what she was referring to but I couldn't say it out loud: the men would rape us. Neither Evin nor I had a precise idea of what that actually meant. In our culture things like that aren't discussed with unmarried women. All we knew is that we'd be defiled, and that we couldn't under any circumstances allow them to touch our bodies. If we failed to prevent them from doing that our entire families would be dishonoured.

'We absolutely have to get out of here before they come back,' I said.

'Sure, but how?' In panic, we looked around the room for a possible way out. Right at the top was a narrow window that wasn't barred. But it was too high to reach without a stool or ladder. In one corner of the room was a whole pile of junk. Maybe there was something in it, which could help us get up to the window or break the lock on the door. We had to search it. 'Quick, help untie me!' I told Evin, holding out my arms.

She yanked at the knots. But as her hands were tied too, it was extremely hard for her to do anything. Her tugging only chafed my wrists. 'It's not working,' she said. 'They've tied the knots too tightly.'

'But it *is* working!' I said, urging her to keep going.

'Doesn't it hurt?'

'I can't feel it at all.'

Finally she managed to loosen the knots enough for me to move my hands at least partially. I rummaged through the pile, which was all stuff the last family had left behind: pots and pans, video cassettes, empty cardboard boxes, an iron, a toy train set. But then I happened upon something useful: an iron rod, about as long as a kebab skewer, but thicker and more solid. I suspected it had belonged to the stove. 'Look!' I said to Evin.

'What is it?'

'No idea. But maybe we can use it to break open the door?'

'How's that going to work?'

I tried to push the rod into the gap between the door and the hinge. But it was too fat. It did, however, fit beneath the door. 'We've got to try and get leverage,' I fantasised. Evin watched me sceptically as I tried pushing the rod upwards on our side of the door. Sheer despair made me try pointless things. The door didn't budge a centimetre, of course; all that happened was that the rod bent slightly.

At that moment we heard the sound of an engine outside, soon followed by footsteps on the stairs. The men were back. But judging by the footsteps and voices there were more than two of them. Now they opened the door to the apartment. Frantically I searched for somewhere to hide the rod, and hurriedly slipped it into the sleeve of my blouse. They entered the apartment and dumped something heavy in the hallway.

Then the door to our room opened. There stood Abu Afram and Eleas, as well as another ISIS man, who had brought Lena and Amna from our former prison. The two of them stood absolutely terrified in the hallway. The men had also bought carpets and bedclothes: all new, but very cheap. They unrolled a carpet with red-and-blue curlicues. The Iraqi carried a second one upstairs. 'Just to make it a bit cosier here, girls,' he said jovially.

The man who'd brought Lena and Amna left again. After carefully bolting the door behind him, they asked us cheerfully to come into the 'kitchen', or rather what was left of it. We were each given a bottle of orange juice, as a welcome drink, so to speak. They were clearly very confident that we had no chance of escaping. They even untied our hands to make it easier for us to drink. When Abu Afram saw the sores on my wrists he said, 'Oh, what's this? Has our wild child been up to her silly tricks again? We'll soon knock that out of you.' He laughed.

I acted as if I couldn't understand a word. I didn't take a sip of the orange juice, either, because I was convinced the Libyan had mixed drugs into the drink, drugs to sedate us. It was like a cup of poison, which you shouldn't touch in any circumstances. While my friends took slow, cautious sips, I racked my brains desperately to work out what we could do to get out of this. Because now it was crystal clear what their intentions were; the men's good spirits confirmed all our worst fears.

When Evin and Amna had finished their drinks, Abu Afram ordered them to go upstairs and wait for him and his colleague. Evin, who was standing right next to me, gave me a look of despair. It broke my heart; I wanted so much to help her.

All of a sudden I had an idea. I stretched my arm out behind my back and let the iron rod slide out. Without their noticing I handed it to my friend, who immediately hid it beneath her veil.

'You can clobber him with it,' I whispered to her in Kurdish.

'Don't worry, I'll kill him before he can do anything,' she whispered back. The men hadn't noticed a thing.

'Come on, come on, hurry up!' Abu Afram harassed them. There was impatience in the Libyan's eyes. He looked like a starving predator. I could virtually smell his lust for sex, which I found utterly repulsive. Everything, absolutely everything about this man was hideous.

Evin obediently went up the stairs, probably because she wanted to avoid them discovering her weapon, the iron rod. But the other girl, Amna, stayed stock-still as if hypnotised, until Abu Afram gave her a slap and dragged her with force to the stairs. Eleas helped him haul her up. Tears of fury and despair ran down Amna's face. But of course she didn't have the strength to resist these two men.

No sooner had Eleas taken Amna upstairs than he came back down to hustle us into the room I'd been locked in with Evin earlier. Now the new carpet was on the floor, as well as the bedclothes. I clutched my bottle of orange juice as I entered the room. 'Make yourselves comfortable. We'll be down for you soon,' he said, before locking the door from the outside. We were trapped.

Lena and I didn't say anything to each other. We didn't share the same bond of trust that existed between Evin and me, so there wasn't anything to say anyway. I didn't know how she felt. But at that terrible moment I had the sense of being all alone in the world. I wasn't really aware of Lena sitting next to me on the rug. And this meant I heard even more acutely the sounds of struggle and despair coming from above. My beloved Evin screamed as if her throat were being slit. It was unbearable. I was so desperate to help her, but there was nothing I could do.

Determined to put an end to the horror, I smashed on the floor the bottle of orange juice I'd brought from the kitchen. Lena watched me, probably thinking that I was planning to use the broken bottle to defend myself when the men came for us. 'We'll kill them,' she said, showing me that she still had her bottle too. But I knew this was impossible. With our improvised weapons the two of us were as little a match for the men as Evin and Amna upstairs.

There was only way to avoid being violated: death. That's why I decided to put an end to my life. It was the only option left to me to save my honour and the honour of my family. I thought of my father, who'd always taught us children that moral and religious values were the most important things to defend. 'Everything else in life is of secondary importance,' he told us. At this time I didn't know whether my father was still alive. But that was irrelevant. I would stick to his principles anyway. If my family found out they'd surely be very proud of me. And even if they were never to know, it was still the right decision, as I would go to my death pure and unsullied. This thought filled me with a profound sense of inner peace.

So I got under the sheet, pretending to go to sleep. Lena lay down beside me. She had no idea what I had in mind. I felt for the broken glass next to me. Picking out the sharpest fragment, I brought it to my left wrist. Calmly and purposefully, I pressed the shard into my skin and jerked it across. I immediately felt the blood spurt out. Quickly I transferred the piece of glass to my other hand; before I passed out I wanted to sever my right artery as well. Strangely, I behaved in a perfectly normal manner, like a doctor carrying out an amputation. I still maintain today that I felt no pain at all.

Soon I was overcome by dizziness, and a pleasant feeling of numbness spread throughout my body. Apparently I was losing a lot of blood. Now Lena realised that something was not right. 'You've gone all pale. What's happening?' she asked anxiously.

Then she saw that the sheet I was beneath was drenched in blood. 'Help!' she screamed. 'Come quickly! Farida's trying to kill herself!'

My last thought was 'Hopefully the men won't hear her'. Then I lost consciousness and don't recall anything more.

I woke up somewhere unfamiliar. Again I was lying on a carpet on the floor, but I'd never seen the room before. It was very clean, almost sterile, you could say, with whitewashed walls, and just a chest of drawers and an armchair for furniture. I was on a crisp white sheet. I was wearing only a pair of knickers and vest, which weren't mine. Sitting beside me on the rug was Evin. Her hand was on my chest and she was looking at me with troubled eyes.

'Farida,' she said. 'Farida, can you hear me?'

'Yes,' I replied. 'Yes, Evin.' She began to cry. Her tears fell onto my face and the bandages that I only now noticed were around my wrists. 'Farida, my dearest Farida, I'm so happy you're awake!' she sobbed. 'Never leave me again.'

'Where are we?' I asked. I was still completely disorientated. 'What happened?'

'You know what happened: you tried to kill yourself,' Evin said, now with a tone of reproach in her voice. She told me how she and the men had heard Lena's cries for help and rushed down the stairs. The men had unlocked the door and found me in a pool of blood. I was already unconscious by then. 'Farida, you were going to leave me on my own! How could you do that to me?'

'I had to – you know why,' I said weakly. And all of a sudden I was seized by a sense of horror. 'Did Abu Afram . . . ?' I couldn't utter the words. 'I mean, did he do anything to me while I was unconscious?'

'No,' Evin said, setting my mind at rest. 'You are untouched.'

'What about you?' I asked apprehensively.

Evin assured me that everything was all right with her too. Abu Afram was about to rape her, but stopped when he heard Lena screaming below. I didn't know whether to believe her account or not. I recalled only too well the scuffles and horrific sounds coming from above, which had driven me to despair. 'You saved me, Farida,' Evin asserted, and I didn't probe any further. I was just happy to know she was near me and very willing to believe that the two of us had remained untouched.

'Thank the Lord for having protected both of us.'

'All the same, you must never do that again. You're never to leave me alone. Will you promise me that?'

I swore faithfully to keep that promise. 'I'll never desert you again.' As I said these words I began to cough. I noticed that not only my throat, but my whole body was dreadfully dehydrated. I saw a carafe of water on the nearby chest of drawers. 'Evin, can you please give me some water?'

'The doctor says you shouldn't drink anything. It's better not to because of the bleeding.'

'Which doctor?' I asked in surprise. Had Abu Afram taken me to a hospital? Where I was looked more like a guest room in a private apartment. 'Where are we, anyway?'

'We're in a doctor's house,' Evin said. 'Abu Afram took us to him. He and his wife are looking after you.'

'Oh, how kind of them.'

But Evin didn't see it quite so positively. 'They're helping him because they belong to his organisation.'

It took me a moment to understand what she was saying. 'So they're ISIS people?'

'Yes,' she confirmed.

My heart sank. I realised now that we weren't free, but still in the hands of people who regarded us as subhuman. They were making me better, but why? Were they going to deliver me back to Abu Afram when I was well again?

I wasn't able to ask Evin this question, for at that moment the door opened and the doctor's wife came in. She was wearing a knee-length skirt and a sleeveless T-shirt. Her hair was conspicuously bleached. That was not how I'd imagined an ISIS woman to look. She probably did the same as most Syrian women: in the occupied area they only put on the black full-length cloak when they went out into the street.

For a moment I had hope. A woman like that, who, in her private life at least, was clearly no extremist, would surely sympathise with us if we told her the story of our abduction. Might we be able to convince her to help us? As a woman she must feel that what the men were doing to us was wrong.

But the woman was extremely unfriendly. She barely spoke to Evin and me, and when she did it was only to list the dos and don'ts. 'You must never leave this room, apart from to go to the loo,' she said coldly. 'And don't get any silly ideas; there are guards outside the building, and all our neighbours are ISIS members too. Do you understand?'

Most of the time, however, she limited herself to changing my bandages in silence. I only saw her husband, the doctor, occasionally, usually when he was examining my wounds. He, too, looked strikingly 'normal' and, apart from a little stubble on his chin, nothing like someone who might belong to ISIS. Were all these people opportunists? Was the terror the organisation exerted over them so ruthless that nobody dared resist? I never heard a single word of regret from these collaborators.

For the first couple of days of my stay with the doctor I was very, very weak and unsteady on my legs. I'd lost a lot of blood, which is why I felt permanently dizzy. The bandages around my hands were also a hindrance. For even the slightest movement I needed Evin's help. She held a bottle of water to my lips, when I was allowed to drink again, fed me rice and soup, and supported me when I needed to go to the loo. When the sun rose in the mornings she helped me get up and bow by the window. Together we'd mutter the prayer that our fathers had taught us: 'Amen, amen, amen. Blessed be our religion.'

But my helplessness made me feel very low. I was particularly upset that my frail constitution prevented me from devising any escape plans. For naturally our current situation offered an excellent opportunity to get away. I urged Evin to explore carefully all the possibilities, so that at least she might be able to escape.

For example, there was a large window in our room, from which you could look into the street. Unfortunately it was on the third floor, which meant that you'd probably injure yourself jumping out. But all the same you'd probably survive, and what was a broken leg in return for freedom?, I thought, somewhat irrationally.

'Try it,' I encouraged Evin. 'At some point in the night jump out and by the time they wake up you'll be long gone.'

'What about you?'

'I can't at the moment. But I'll try later on.'

I also offered to distract the doctor and his wife so that she could escape via the door. Normally it was locked. But when they came to check up on me, they left it unlocked. 'I could feign an epileptic attack,' I suggested. 'Then they'll be busy attending to me and you can do a runner. Please have a go, Evin.'

But she rejected all my suggestions. 'I'm not going anywhere without you,' came her categorical reply.

'You'll regret it!'

'I'd regret deserting you much more. I'd never be able to forgive myself, Farida.' Evin had been brought up with the same moral code as I had. For her, too, the ethical principles dictated by our religion were paramount. According to these a betrayal of friendship would be a mortal sin. 'We're staying together,' she said, stroking my wounded hands, 'no matter what happens.'

On the fifth day after my suicide attempt, our respite at the doctor's house came to an abrupt end. His wife put new bandages on for the last time. Although my wounds were still far from healed, clearly her husband thought I no longer needed their care. 'Right then, ladies,' he said, after they'd seen to me. 'That's us done. It's time for us to take you back now.'

Before Evin and I could properly understand what he was saying, he ordered us to veil ourselves and go with him. His wife also veiled herself, just as I had thought, with a black niqab that left just a slit for the eyes, so she could come too, probably to keep an eye on us.

She led us down the stairs and sat between Evin and me when we got into the doctor's white Opel. Once again I was astounded by her; even though she was a woman, she seemed to have no scruples about what happened to us. Was it just because we didn't pray to the same god?

The doctor started the engine and drove the car to one of the suburbs of Raqqa. I noted, with a touch of relief, that it wasn't the district where our Libyan 'owner' and his friend lived. 'Where are you taking us?' Evin asked. But she got no reply.

After about half an hour's drive we arrived in a quiet, secluded residential area. The houses looked intact; this place must have been spared fighting or bombardments. We pulled up at a one-storey house, whose shutters were closed. My heart almost stopped when I saw the four-by-four parked outside. 'That's Abu Afram's car,' I whispered to Evin.

She recognised it too. 'Yes, I fear you're right,' she said.

'But why's he having us brought here?'

'Perhaps he moved?'

We were at a loss, but we didn't have time to think about it any longer. For the doctor was getting out, and then opening the locked door. 'We're here,' he said.

His wife stayed in the car while he took us to the house. Two men were waiting at the door, one of whom we already knew: Abu Afram's friend, Eleas, the fat Iraqi. He handed the doctor a few banknotes, no doubt the remuneration for my treatment. His face was sombre. We'd never seen the second man before. He was a short, likewise very fat Syrian with a bald head. He was wearing normal clothes and didn't have an ISIS beard.

'In you come, my lovelies,' he said.

No sooner were we in the house than the Syrian shut the door behind us. 'Right,' he said to Eleas, 'now you can do what you want with them. Be as rough as you like. But don't forget: I'm buying them as virgins!'

'Don't worry. I just want to give them a little lesson,' he replied. He stood in front of us, menacingly. 'Abu Afram is very, very angry with you,' he snarled. 'What on earth were you thinking? Do you honestly believe we'd let you spoil our fun?'

Trembling, we waited for what was coming. Evin shuffled up close to me.

'I'm going to show you your place, you little Yazidi sluts!'

I saw him lunge at me with the bottle of water in his hand. I tried in vain to defend myself with my bound arms. The bottle crashed against my head, leaving me reeling. Then he came closer and rammed his fist into my stomach. I sank to the floor. But he wasn't finished yet; he hit and punched me repeatedly as I lay there.

Then he turned to Evin and beat her too. This may sound incomprehensible for people who've grown up in a different culture, but I can't hide the fact that, in a way, it pleased me. For his fury at Evin proved to me that she hadn't been lying. She must have succeeded in preventing the worst, thereby denting Abu Afram's pride. Otherwise there was no reason to take it out on her so brutally. In truth, I was rejoicing inside; we'd done it! And we'd do it again. We'd take a stand against these men.

The Iraqi thrashed Evin until she crumpled to the floor. He really wanted to hurt us badly, and kept punching us in the stomach. But he didn't touch us sexually.

Once he'd finished venting his anger and we lay whimpering on the ground, the Iraqi took his leave of the Syrian with the words, 'They're all yours now. Have fun!' Then he vanished, slamming the door behind him.

The Syrian unlocked a room and ordered us to go in. With great difficulty Evin managed to get on all fours and crawl in that direction. But I was in such a bad state that I couldn't move, so he took me by both arms and dragged me in.

It was a tiny room with a shabby brown leather sofa and two even shabbier foam mattresses. The bald man laid me down on one of these. I was vaguely aware that there were other girls in the room. 'Farida!' said one of them, who obviously knew me. But I was so disorientated after the beating that I couldn't place her. 'That's Farida, our maths genius!'

Then I realised that all the girls in the room were school friends of mine: Nuhat, our chemistry expert; Revin, our shy class poet; as well as Lava and Khamia, who were a little younger and had always been the life and soul of the playground. I'd last seen them at the slave market in Raqqa; like Evin and myself they'd all been sold to various men. I was astonished to see them here again.

The Syrian turned off the light in the room and locked the door from the outside. All of a sudden it was pitch-black. So this was our new prison, a dark hole, I thought, as dark as my soul.

Evin felt for me with her hand. 'Are you OK, Farida?' she asked when she'd found me.

'Yes,' I lied, even though I felt wretched. The blows to my stomach had achieved their desired effect: I had to throw up. Evin held up my head as I was sick.

'I'm really sorry,' I mumbled.

'It's all right,' she said, stroking my forehead.

She put my head in her lap. For a while she just sat there, continuing to stroke me. I gradually calmed down. 'Where have we ended up?' I asked feebly.

'This is Abu Dua's house,' the other girls said. 'He bought you.' We learned that all the girls in the room had been sold on by their 'owners'.

'Does he need so many women?'

'No, he's a dealer,' they explained. 'He buys and sells women.'

So we were in the house of a professional women trafficker, or to be more precise, a middleman in the women-trafficking business. Abu Dua didn't acquire Yazidi slaves for his own use, but to sell them on for a profit. At first I didn't know whether to take this as good or bad news, but then I decided it might be an advantage. The fact that the Syrian hadn't bought us for himself gave us a breathing space at least. If we could make use of this to escape we might be able to avoid being violated after all.

I resolved that as soon as I was able I'd make a detailed study of our new prison, in an attempt to identify the weak spot in the system. At Evin's side I fell into a fitful sleep.

When I woke up it was still dark. My vomit was still on Evin's skirt and it stank horribly. Nothing had changed. But I felt very hungry and thirsty. How long had we been in Abu Dua's house? I wondered. Hours? A whole day, perhaps? I didn't know. I didn't even know whether it was night or day.

Eventually the door opened and the light went on. We screwed up our eyes. The Syrian came over to us. We recoiled, still anticipating the worst. But he was only bringing us cheese sandwiches and water. My body was desperate for food and liquid, which is why I forgot my pride and greedily devoured the two sandwiches which were my ration, and gulped the water from the plastic bottle.

How should I describe Abu Dua's behaviour towards us? He treated us like animals in a cage; he didn't care in the slightest what it was like for us in our dark prison. All he did was ensure that we didn't die of hunger or thirst. We could only go to the loo under his supervision; he would accompany each girl one by one to the door. Because of the state we were in, however, he allowed Evin and me to go together and help each other.

The room consisted of just a tap, a boiler and a concrete latrine hole. It had no window to the outside. My friend washed her skirt under the tap and dabbed the black eye Eleas had given me with a damp corner of her veil. As she looked at me sadly, I could almost hear what she was thinking: how had the two of us got into this degrading situation? How could it have happened, seeing as only a few weeks ago we were still leading perfectly normal lives? Although we were grateful to have each other close, there are some things in life you don't want anyone else to witness. And such was the situation we were in. I think we were both ashamed at the other seeing us look so terrible, so wretched. But there was nothing we could do about it. Life itself had laid this burden on us.

We were swamped by the darkness surrounding us. Only a weak shimmer that sometimes seeped through the chinks between the window and the permanently closed shutters allowed us to tell whether the sun was shining outside, in the other world. But for us the time of day did not exist, only a vague sense that Abu Dua came twice daily to bring us our cheese sandwiches; nothing else was on the menu. Most of the time, however, the six of us would sleep closely huddled on the mattresses. There wasn't anything else to do.

Except dream. Occasionally, when the time dragged, we'd recall the life we'd left behind in Kocho. 'Do you think the roses are still flowering in your garden?' Evin said to me. And instantly I saw in my mind my mother's flower beds and the perfume of the flowers tickled my nostrils. I was overcome by a surge of longing.

'Normally they don't come into bloom until August,' I said.

'And it's not autumn yet.'

'No.' I found this thought comforting somehow. Would we get back home before autumn arrived? Would the roses flower then? 'But if no one's watering them they'll have dried up long ago.'

'Why do you talk like that?' Evin said. 'I bet our families have returned to Kocho by now.'

'Yes, for sure,' I acquiesced, thinking of my mother. Where was she now? What about my brothers? Were they all right? In silence each of us wallowed in our own thoughts.

The other girls said nothing to us about what had happened with their first 'owners'. And we didn't talk about our experiences either. All of us found it embarrassing to talk about anything to do with sex. We couldn't bring ourselves to do it even in this very particular situation.

But Evin and I soon discovered that one of the girls here was having an even harder time than the rest of us: Nuhat. My shy, slightly chubby classmate with the pale button nose and long brown hair had been picked out by Abu Dua for his own use. After distributing the sandwiches and accompanying us to the bathroom, he often took her out while the rest of us remained sitting in our dark cell. Shortly afterwards we'd hear her screams coming from one of the other rooms.

'Poor Nuhat,' Evin said.

'We're not going to have it any better,' Revin said. Abu Dua had recently told her that he'd earmarked her for his friend Abu Hassan. 'He's a good man,' he'd said. 'I hope you'll prove worthy of him. Otherwise he'll end up bringing you back to me!' With a laugh he'd slapped her on the shoulder while she'd stood there, petrified.

When Nuhat returned to us in the prison after her time with Abu Dua she looked similarly shell-shocked. Sometimes she shed silent tears of fury too. But she never said a word about what he did to her. And we didn't ask; the shame was too great.

Abu Dua lived alone in the house. I didn't know where his family was; at any rate we didn't hear any other voices in the house. Only once did he get a visit, from the Iraqi Eleas, who'd beaten Evin and me. The men were evidently friends and had arranged to meet for tea. Eleas did not arrive alone, however, but in the company of a woman, as we worked out from the greetings exchanged in the hallway. Then the door opened suddenly, the light went on and we had a visitor too.

In spite of what she was wearing I knew the woman wrapped in black. It was the girl who'd lain beside me when I slit my wrists. 'Lena!' I cried, when she came in. 'Is it really you?'

Removing the veil from her face, she smiled when she recognised me. 'Farida! You're alive! Thank the Lord! You gave us all a terrible fright.'

I gave an impatient shrug. 'Are you still with him?'

'As you can see,' she said, sitting down beside us on the mattress. I have to admit that she didn't look that bad. However, the dazzling neon light all of a sudden flooding the room, which was normally pitch-black, unsettled me and the other girls. It was strange to receive a visitor in such surroundings.

'What about your plan to kill him?' I asked.

'It failed.' She told us how she had actually tried to smash the bottle over his head. But he'd overpowered her. This must have happened when Abu Afram had driven Evin and me to the doctor's house. She sounded despondent as she recalled that night. 'I was terribly envious of you, Farida,' she said. 'But I wasn't as strong as you. He made me his wife.'

'His regular wife? Does that mean you've become a Muslim too?' I probed.

'Only a pretend one,' she assured us. 'Only a pretend one.' Lena seemed embarrassed by what she was saying, for she could sense that the rest of us were rather affronted. 'It's just a strategy, you understand? At some point, when the time's right, I'm going to escape from him.'

'Everyone has to find the way that suits them,' I said, lost in thought, my gaze alighting on the windows. For the first time I had the opportunity to have a proper look in the light at how they were secured. I noted that Abu Dua had wound steel wire around the handle at the bottom of one of them. Behind the windows were the permanently closed shutters. He'd probably secured them from the outside.

'The most important thing is that none of us gives up our search for a way to freedom,' I told Lena. She agreed with me. Later I discovered that she did actually try to run away from Eleas, but was captured again. As far as I know she must still be living with him.

We tried to flee the house that very same night.

'Did you see?' I asked Evin and the other girls when Lena had gone and we were sitting in darkness once more. 'That window is only fastened with wire.'

The others understood immediately what I was getting at. 'Do you think we'd be able to open it? And what about the shutter on the other side?'

'We'll find out,' I said. 'Let's try at least. In any case, his construction doesn't seem particularly sturdy.'

I felt for the handle and the wire. In fact, Abu Dua seemed to have tied it very skilfully, because I couldn't find a beginning or an end. Without any light it was hard to do, just feeling with my hands. Perhaps I'd been mistaken and his security system worked better than I'd thought.

But then, under my little finger I felt something sharp: the end of the wire! In great excitement I traced its course with my finger. The wire was twisted round a number of times. Abu Dua had secured it very carefully, but still not carefully enough. With no little patience and by feeling with the tips of my fingers I was able to loosen the knots and free the handle.

'I've done it!' I said softly. My heart was thumping euphorically. All my fellow prisoners crowded around me. In total darkness I pushed up the window and we breathed in the fresh night-time breeze, which blew in through the gaps in the wood of the shutter. It was a massive moment. Now all that separated us from freedom was a window shutter!

I felt the wood, to the bottom of which another metal handle was attached, and tried pushing the shutter up too. But it wouldn't budge. I gave it a good shake. 'Not so loud!' Evin warned me.

'But I've got to get it open,' I said in my defence. 'What else do you expect me to do?'

I shook it even harder, and even more noisily. We heard the door being unlocked from the other side. Abu Dua switched on the light and saw the six of us gathered around the open window. We stared at him as if we'd seen a ghost. 'What are you brats up to?' he yelled.

'We just wanted a bit of fresh air. It's so sticky in here,' Evin stammered.

'Do you really think you can take me for a ride like that?' He gave my friend a resounding slap. But she didn't wince. 'You don't behave like that with me, bitch! Do you understand?'

Abu Dua was in a blind rage. He threatened to hit all the other girls too. But first he had a more important task. He fetched his drill and began to fortify the window as securely as possible, by mounting a bracket on the wall, which he connected to the window handle with a large padlock.

'Right, that's enough fresh air nonsense,' he said grimly. 'And mark my words: if you try that again I'll sell you to the worst men I know. The very worst.'

Nobody said a word. We were all intimidated by his threat. But more crucially, yet another hope had been snuffed out.

The following day two men came to see Abu Dua: customers wanting to buy girls. In the room next door we heard heated negotiations and haggling.

In our prison we grew increasingly nervous. We knew that the men would want to take someone away with them. It couldn't be Nuhat, as presumably Abu Dua intended to keep her for himself. And supposedly Revin was already promised to his friend, although you never knew how much this was dependent on the price, ultimately. So theoretically, at least, that left Lava, Khamia, Evin and me. We pressed our ears to the wall, but couldn't really make out what was being said. We only picked out scraps of the conversation: 'young girls', 'sale', 'virgins', 'large breasts'.

'Who are they talking about?' I whispered to Evin.

'I don't think they've made their minds up.'

At some point the door opened. 'Lava, Khamia,' Abu Dua called. 'Come with me!'

The two girls crawled into the corners of the room. But of course there was nowhere for them to hide. I saw them shaking with fear and felt very sorry for them. I recalled how at school they'd always been bubbling with joy. But they'd been robbed of all this by their time as ISIS prisoners. Now they cowered there like scared animals. 'I told you both to come with me right away!' Abu Dua ordered, drawing out his words menacingly. 'Hurry up!'

Taking a step closer, he gave both of them a slap. They started crying. But Abu Dua grabbed both of them by the arm. 'Why do you always have to make such a song and dance about it? What effect do you think it has on the customers?' the bald man grumbled, hauling them out of the room. 'You're behaving like children!' Yes, I thought. That's what they were.

When the door was closed again, Evin and I took a deep breath. It's mean to say it, but of course we were relieved that it hadn't been our turn this time. I expect the buyers had been put off by our ages. They always wanted very young girls, as had been the case at the slave market in Raqqa, where the youngest were always the first to go. At around fourteen years old, Lava and Khamia were the youngest in our group. But maybe the price that Abu Dua had asked for Evin and me as virgins was simply not right for them.

In the room next door we heard the whistles and lewd comments the potential buyers made as Lava and Khamia were paraded before them. Seemingly they liked what they saw. A deal was reached and our two friends left the house, putting up the greatest possible resistance. But it didn't help them one bit.

Abu Dua came back into the house whistling, as pleased as Punch. He must have struck a good deal.

He went to the loo and then came into us, demanding Nuhat and Revin. The two of them were going to be taken immediately to another room, he said. Their heads bowed, they followed him out.

I felt terrible. I could feel the pressure increasing in my head, which normally heralded an attack. But I tried to calm myself, for I knew that a clear head was the only thing that could help us. 'Evin,' I said, 'we've got to get out of here – urgently!'

'Yes, I know,' she replied. Neither of us said what we were both thinking: now that Lava and Khamia had gone, we would inevitably be the next ones that Abu Dua, the people trafficker, sold to some rogues. Which meant time really was of the essence. Think, Farida, I commanded myself. There had to be a way out of this cursed hole!

The only thing that occurred to me was the window again. I felt for the bracket that Abu Dua had screwed into the wall and gave it a shake. Perhaps it was loose and might come away from the wall, I thought. But it didn't move one millimetre.

'Maybe you could try the other window,' Evin suddenly suggested.

I was thunderstruck. Yes, of course! There was the other window! In the heat of the moment Abu Dua hadn't fixed a lock to that one. The handle must be behind the sofa. Why didn't we think of this before?

The two of us pushed the sofa forward a little. It moved with a grinding sound. 'Not too loud!' Evin warned me. But this time we were lucky. At that moment Abu Dua was too busy with Nuhat to pay attention to the noises in the house.

I felt for the handle. It seemed to be the same wire system he'd used on the other window. 'Abu Dua must think we're stupid!' I said in triumph, getting to work on the knot straight away.

'Maybe it's him who's stupid,' Evin giggled. 'These men have only got one thing on their minds.'

I'd soon dealt with the wire. Now opening the window was a piece of cake. All that remained was the rolling shutter. I tried pushing it up, and managed to move it a centimetre. But then it stopped as if there was resistance somewhere. 'I think he must have secured it outside,' I said, disheartened.

'Maybe it's just stuck,' Evin said. 'Let me have a go.'

We joined forces and managed to shift it a few centimetres more. 'The wood's warped,' Evin said. She suspected that it had been exposed to the weather for too long. 'Rain can have this effect.' So we kept trying, pushing and shoving as hard as we could.

'We've got to do it, we *have* to,' I kept saying. I was convinced our lives depended on it. Not to mention our honour.

'Let's hope he doesn't catch us a second time,' Evin said nervously. Taking turns, we finally managed to heave the stubborn shutter about twenty-five centimetres upwards. We hadn't opened up much more than a chink. Through it we could see the dark street – our freedom. Our chance to escape the horror.

As soon as we were able to get our heads through the gap we tried to climb out. Evin went first. I kept pushing her, until she could support herself with her hands on the asphalt outside. Then she did a sort of flip and landed on her feet on the trafficker's veranda. I chucked her our black cloaks.

Then it was my turn. I couldn't tumble out as acrobatically as Evin, as the scars on my knuckles were still too raw to put that sort of strain on them. So Evin pulled me out by my arms and I landed on my belly. But I didn't care; the main thing was that we were free!

'We've done it!' I whispered, hardly able to believe it. 'We're out!' An overwhelming feeling of joy pulsed through my body. I swiftly put on the Islamic clothing so we wouldn't be stopped and locked up again straight away.

'Quick, let's go,' Evin urged. 'Let's get out of here before Abu Dua –'

She got no further. For at that moment the Syrian appeared on his veranda in a dressing gown. He flicked his lighter to light a cigarette. As we knew, he liked to smoke one after abusing Nuhat.

When he saw our shadowy figures by the window his eyes practically popped out of his head. 'You damned devil children,' he bellowed. 'Didn't I tell you it wouldn't end well? Stay right where you are!' But we blundered away. 'Stop them!' I could hear Abu Dua cry out behind us.

We ran towards the wooden fence surrounding his property. But we didn't get far. Two ISIS soldiers who were keeping guard at the nearby crossroads ran towards us and stopped us in our tracks. Abu Dua caught up with us. 'These are my Yazidis,' he wheezed.

'Can you prove that?' the bearded men asked.

'Of course,' he affirmed. 'I've got the ownership papers.'

As Abu Dua sorted out the formalities with the ISIS men, they put us in handcuffs and took us back to our prison. 'Keep a closer eye on them in future!' they advised him, laughing.

Scarcely was our 'owner' alone with us than he flew into a rage and started beating us. 'So, think you can make a fool out of me, do you? I'd already heard about the two of you; you're really insufferable. But now you'll go somewhere that you'll never escape from!'

After giving us a sound thrashing, he whipped out his mobile phone and dialled a number. 'Emir Zeyad? *Salam alaikum!*' The men exchanged a few pleasantries. Then Abu Dua came to the point. 'You told me to get in touch when I had some virgins for sale.' Evin and I exchanged worried glances. 'Yes, two: eighteen and twenty-four years old . . . A little old? . . . Ha ha, yes, I know, but they're hot and feisty. Look, I'll make you a special offer.' He darted vicious glances at Evin and me. 'Perfect. See you in a couple of hours.' Abu Dua ended the call.

'You'll be begging to come back here,' he predicted.

And unfortunately he was right, because Abu Dua had sold us to the chief of the Bater – or 'Beasts' – division in the Syrian desert.

6

WITH THE 'BEASTS'

Abu Dua no longer let us out of his sight. Evin and I had hoped that he'd send us back to the dark room where we'd sat tight for almost ten days. But he didn't fancy taking any more risks with us. 'Girls like you are bad for business; I should never have bought you,' he said, sitting opposite and watching over us until we were picked up. Our wrists were still shackled. 'I'm not playing Mr Nice Guy any more,' said the trafficker. 'Now the two of you will realise where your stubbornness gets you.'

After some time a car turned into the drive. Libyan ISIS men in military clothing got out. These were soldiers of Commander Omar Zeyad, who was also called the 'Emir'. After they'd sorted out the business formalities with Abu Dua, they pointed their machine guns at us and ordered us to get into the military vehicle. Although we knew there was no point in putting up a struggle, we did make a last desperate attempt to run away before they hauled us into the car. Evin and I both agreed that anything was better than being handed over to their master; we'd far rather be shot. But they declined to do us this favour.

The men caught us without much difficulty and shackled us to the back seat with our handcuffs. Then the car raced through the pitch-black night into the desert, leaving Raqqa behind. The air blew back to us through the half-opened windows. The men were listening to an MP3 recording of surahs from the Quran, totally indifferent to our whimpers and moans.

At some point, perhaps around midnight, we reached the Euphrates and the city of Deir ez-Zor, which at the time was controlled by ISIS. We drove to a suburb; I saw 'She-Hadad' written on a sign. The local ISIS chief, the Libyan Emir Zeyad, was waiting for us in a dark two-storey building.

The commander of the 'Beasts' was talking to a group of subordinates when we were taken into his house. Zeyad was a not particularly tall man, with long hair and a beard streaked with grey. He had coarse facial features, a broad jaw and wore the typical black ISIS uniform. From the outset his appearance frightened me. When he saw us struggling as we were led to him, a broad smile spread across his face. 'That's enough for today,' he said to his men.

He ordered everyone apart from his deputy, Galib, and a few guards to leave the house and go to bed. For his deputy, a tall, dark-skinned type with short stubble, the invitation to stay was clearly an honour. At any rate, he thanked his friend and superior profusely. 'It's time we had a little fun now,' Emir Zeyad told him.

I can't put into words what I felt at that moment. Obviously I knew what their intentions were and also that there was nothing I could do to prevent it. I saw Evin and me standing shackled before these two men, and yet somehow wasn't present. I evaded their gaze, instead staring at a pot on one of the carpets, which contained some leftovers. It must have been what remained of a communal dinner. Who made it? I wondered. Another slave, maybe? Or one of their wives?

I recalled the meals I'd cooked for my family back home. I wasn't hungry; at that moment I felt no physical needs at all. I focused on the pot only because it was a sort of anchor point for me, connecting me to another world. A world in which rice was cooked and people sat down together in the evenings to eat in peace. Yes, that world did exist, I thought. And it still existed. At some point, however, I'd been expelled from that world and catapulted into another.

Now I was in a world dominated by war and where I would be the victim of violence. I knew it was a terrible mistake. I didn't belong here. And yet my body, at least, was trapped in this place and unable to escape it for the time being.

Only my soul was able to roam freely, hovering somewhere above the room with the two Libyans. The men who were intending to rape Evin and me.

'What's she staring like that for?' Galib asked.

'No idea. They say she's a bit crazy, but sweet. I'll take her,' the Emir said. 'I'll let you have the other one.'

Galib voiced his gratitude again. It was evident that neither he nor his chief had any scruples about giving away another human being or accepting one as a gift. For them we were objects to be used for their pleasure, and which could be bought, sold or swapped as they liked. It was a custom among the soldiers to offer a woman as a reward for particular achievements. Our feelings had no bearing on the matter.

They pushed us towards the bathroom. 'You stink!' they cried. 'Why do all Yazidi girls have to smell so bad? Go on, have a shower!'

We resisted as best we could with handcuffs on. 'We don't want to shower,' Evin said. Since our abduction she and I had realised that it was advantageous to appear as repulsive as possible, because that way we became less desirable as sex objects. This is why we never washed. What's more, we were still wearing the same clothes we'd had on when they took us away a month before; we'd been wearing them day and night. No surprise, then, that we smelled dreadful. But it was naive to think that this could stop the men from executing their plan.

'Oh yes you are going to shower, you stinking Yazidi whores!' they yelled, slapping us as hard as they could in the face. But I have to say that I didn't feel a thing. My only thought was how we could possibly extricate ourselves from this situation.

There was just one way out: I had to kill myself. I'd promised Evin never to leave her alone, and I wouldn't break this promise. We would depart our bodies and this terrible world together. For there was no other option to escape being violated. I needed a weapon, though, and my eyes zealously scanned the room for an appropriate tool.

The men ripped off our veils and yanked us to the bathroom by our hair. We kicked and screamed. We screamed so loudly that the entire neighbourhood must have heard. But no one bothered about what went on in the Emir's house at night. Only when they'd locked the door did they remove our handcuffs.

'Get undressed!' they barked. Of course we did nothing of the sort.

They whipped out daggers from their belts. With a swift cut from top to bottom Emir Zeyad deprived me of my skirt and blouse.

'Now we're going to give the two of you a good scrub,' they announced.

As they shoved us towards the shower I suddenly had an idea. 'The bulb,' I said to Evin in Kurdish. 'Do you see the bulb above the shower? I'll make a short circuit.' So we could take our lives. 'Agreed?'

'Agreed,' she replied in tears.

We allowed ourselves to be pushed under the shower. Evin held me tight. When the men turned on the water my arm shot upwards. I took out the bulb. It went dark. As fast as I could I tried to stick my finger in. But the men yanked me away.

'Stop that nonsense!' Zeyad bellowed, as he pressed me to the floor with all his weight.

Galib opened the bathroom door, allowing light to come in again. The water was still running. One of the guards brought a gas lamp and went away again, so his chiefs could continue with their game undisturbed. 'You bloody whore!' Zeyad cursed. 'I'll soon teach you who's in charge here!'

The men were both drenched too now, but undeterred. I observed myself as if from a distance, calmly imagining that the girl enduring all of this only looked like me. She was my doppelgänger. I, the real Farida, was floating above her, where the men couldn't reach me.

I watched them haul us up the stairs and shunt us into a room laid out with expensive rugs. There were also new clothes for us to put on: a red dress for Evin and one in two different shades of blue for me. We hurriedly got dressed.

Trembling, we crept into a corner of the room, hoping that it was all over. Perhaps the men had just been having a bit of fun with us.

But they came in after us.

When we awoke the following morning on two shabby mattresses, our bodies were burning and aching. The smell of blood and sperm clung to the dresses that Evin and I were still wearing from the night before. We felt such shame that we could barely look each other in the eye.

The room we were in was very small, hot and sticky. There was only one window, high up, secured inside with a lattice of thin, close-meshed wire, and outside with thick, robust metal bars. The door was securely locked too. We hammered against it, but when we heard footsteps approach we immediately felt frightened.

The door opened and an armed ISIS fighter stood before us, probably one of Zeyad's guards. 'What is it?' he snapped.

'We're desperate for the loo,' we said.

'OK, come with me.'

He led us across a gloomy hallway to the loo. I wanted to relieve myself. But it was almost impossible. When I tried my entire abdomen felt as if it were on fire. I think it was the same with Evin. But rather than say anything to me she just cried quietly to herself.

I tried to wash using the tap. For the first time since being taken prisoner I felt the need to clean myself and wash away everything that man had left behind. I even held the dress under the tap. Evin did the same. But no matter how hard we scrubbed the feeling remained that we'd never get clean again. Eventually the ISIS guard thought we'd been in there too long and called out, 'Hey, what's taking you so long?'

Before he could open the door himself we came out and let him take us back to our cell. Evin and I huddled silently on the mattresses and withdrew into ourselves. Both of us were alone in our suffering and self-pity on that bleak morning. After being used by the men we felt dirty. Now we were sinful women, women everyone in the village would turn their noses up at. And both of us felt guilty too. Why couldn't we have prevented it? This was possibly the worst thing: the accusations we levelled against ourselves. We did it automatically. I, at least, had been told time and again from a very young age that a woman's honour stood for the honour of her whole family, and so it was my duty to protect it. But I'd failed. Of course I knew that I was not to blame, not directly at least; I'd done everything in my power to stop it. The men had simply been physically stronger. And yet I was tormented by a bad conscience as far as my family was concerned. Hopefully my parents and brothers would never find out what had happened to me, I thought.

I recalled the time when we'd all lived together in our beautiful house with its garden, instinctively recollecting how my brothers would always lurk greedily around the cooker when I was making dinner for them. Then I saw us all sitting around the large table, devouring the delicious kebabs. In my memory my home in Kocho became ever more like an illusion. Had I really lived in this little paradise?

At some point, perhaps it was already the afternoon, our 'owners' came to see us. We heard their footsteps in the hall, and also heard them talking as they approached our cell. 'If that little minx speaks even one word of Arabic I'm going to take her back to Libya,' Zeyad said. My heart almost stopped. So the monster wanted to take me to Libya? Over my dead body, I immediately swore to myself. Only over my dead body would he even touch me again.

I felt ill the moment I saw Zeyad's head in the door and took in his odour. My memory of the previous night returned painfully and I started to quiver. I crept into the farthest corner of the cell, which appeared to amuse him. He followed me and stroked me under the chin with his forefinger. 'So, my little one,' he said, 'how are you feeling today? It wasn't so bad, was it?' He laughed as if he'd just cracked a funny joke.

I spat at him, but only caught his clothes, unfortunately. He wiped away the spit with his hand. 'Don't get cocky,' he said, slapping me. 'Otherwise I'll take you again right now.'

It was meant as a threat. But I can't say that it particularly frightened me at that moment. Something inside me seemed to have died. I didn't react and stared obstinately at the floor. 'Hey, do you understand me?' he said.

'She doesn't speak Arabic,' Evin said.

'Who asked you?'

'She's my sister.'

'So tell me, how come *you* speak such good Arabic then? If she's your sister she must have learned it at school too!'

'I taught myself,' Evin lied. 'From the telly.'

The men wondered whether to believe her. They exchanged uncertain glances, but then let the matter rest. 'Well, tell your little sister that she made me very cross with her silly games last night,' he said, 'and that I'm going to give her a good spanking now.' He loosened his belt in preparation for a thrashing.

'It's not Farida's fault,' my friend said, coming to my defence. 'She's ill.'

At that moment the Emir's mobile buzzed. The Libyan frowned as he checked the display, and took the call. 'What's up?' he asked.

In a loud, overwrought voice, one of his commanders told him about fighting that had broken out somewhere nearby with a rival jihadi group. At once Emir Zeyad was all ears, demanding to know precisely where this was happening and how many men were on the opposing side. 'We'll be right there,' he promised. 'In thirty minutes.'

After ending the call he told Galib, 'We've got to go, this instant. Our boys need help.' He cast me an evil look. 'Don't think you're getting off that easily. The moment we're back you'll get your punishment for last night.'

We breathed a sigh of relief when Zeyad and Galib left the cell. 'I hope those bastards get a bullet in their heads and we never see them again,' I said to Evin.

'Maybe they'll be taken prisoner. That would be the best thing.'

'Let's hope their opponents have a particularly excruciating death in store for them. I'd love them to waste away as painfully as possible.'

We couldn't stop fantasising about the most horrific forms of death we were wishing on our tormentors. This was fuelled by the fact that we didn't in fact see Zeyad and Galib again for several days. The ISIS guard who accompanied us to the loo gave us the bare minimum of food and water. Each evening he came with a bottle with less than half a litre of water and a few biscuits. Apart from him no one bothered about us. I think the room in which we were held captive was on a kind of prison wing, for we never saw anyone in the hallway save for the guard. Or perhaps all the men had gone to fight with the Emir.

We stuck it out in the scorching heat. 'I really think they *have* been shot,' I said to Evin at some point. 'It's possible.'

'Yes, perhaps.' She looked thoughtful. 'What would that mean? What's going to happen to us if they're dead?'

I mulled this over. What, according to ISIS law, happened to a 'slave' whose 'owner' had died? Would we be 'bequeathed' to someone else? Had Zeyad and Galib made provision for this? Later I found out that one of their religious leaders had issued a fatwa regulating these questions. It stipulated that, like all the other 'assets' of our 'owners', we would indeed be divided among his men. But luckily we didn't know this while we were imprisoned in Deir ez-Zor.

As we ruminated we heard shots outside. We listened in anticipation. Had the fighting reached us? For a moment we were hopeful. Perhaps it was the Kurds or even the Americans come to liberate us. But then we heard the words *Allahu akbar* and cries of victory from the men. Our tormentors had obviously won the battle and were probably celebrating outside. Our hearts sank.

Shortly afterwards four men came to fetch us. They brought us both a black full-length cloak and an extra veil for our faces. 'Put that on and follow us,' they ordered. 'Your owners are asking for you.'

When we refused, two men held each of us and forcibly put the cloaks over us. But as we belonged to their chiefs, they took great care to avoid touching us in an inappropriate way, especially with witnesses present. When they'd packaged us up, two of the men took Evin away. I kicked up a fuss, demanding to stay with her; the two remaining men yelled at me to shut up. Then they took me down some stairs and out into the street. I blinked. For the first time in ages I could see the sun again – albeit through the black veil – and I felt its pleasant warmth on my shoulders. Yes, I thought, that other world does still exist. I secretly bowed to the mighty celestial body and begged my Lord Melek Taus to save us. 'Amen, amen, amen,' I whispered.

Taking me by the arm through a chaotic mass of military vehicles and ISIS fighters who'd just returned from the battle, the men led me to a house on the other side of the street. I wondered who it belonged to. Perhaps it was Emir Zeyad's private house, or, more accurately, the house he'd appropriated from someone else. Among all the beards I hadn't noticed him yet.

They shunted me through the entrance and hallway into a bedroom. Yes, it was a perfectly normal, homely bedroom. It had a double bed, a wardrobe full of clothes that the original owners must have left behind, and a large mirror in which I saw myself as a dark ghost. My eyes staring through the slit were unnaturally wide. I couldn't stand the way I looked and quickly averted my gaze.

'Get ready,' the men told me. 'The Emir will be with you very soon.' Then they went out, carefully locking the door behind them.

I was perfectly calm and thought about the options still open to me. I didn't doubt for one minute that after the victorious battle Zeyad would be in the mood for a woman. He'd had me brought here to rape me again. There was no reason to assume any different.

So what was I to do? I couldn't just wait for him to come and inflict more pain on me, even though it wasn't the pain that horrified me most; it was the idea that this man was satisfying his desires with me, that he was using me. No, I would not allow that to happen a second time.

Looking around the room, I caught sight of a hook in the ceiling. The fan, which had probably once been attached to it, was missing. Perfect! A hook, a veil, I calculated coolly, what else did I need to take my own life? This time I wasn't thinking of escape. Although there was a window, I didn't even entertain the idea that I might use it to get away. I was just too depressed for a cunning plan like that. I lacked the energy and the confidence. For now that I'd lost my honour, what use was taking flight? I'd only bring disgrace on my parents. It would be better if I was dead.

So, taking the veil from my head, I climbed onto the bed and tied it firmly with a knot to the hook. I can't say I was sad when I put the noose around my neck. My life was no longer worth feeling sorry about. I felt extraordinarily lonely. What a shame not to be able to say goodbye to my parents at least. Would they ever know what I had done? Would they be proud of me? How about Evin? Would they show her my body? Would she be angry with me? No, I decided, Evin would understand me better than anyone else in the world. Goodbye, world! Goodbye, dear friend! Look after yourself, Evin!

I leapt, yanking down the veil, and hit my head on the side of the bed. I felt a stinging pain before passing out.

Later, when I awoke, Evin told me that the Emir had been irate when he brought me back. He must have come into the room soon afterwards and found me on the floor. He'd carried me across the street wrapped in the black cloth, and of course all his subordinates had seen what had happened: I'd thwarted their chief's plans. So the Emir was in a foul mood when he dumped me next to Evin in the prison. In spite of the injury to my head, he didn't consider any medical treatment.

Evin had cleaned the cut on my head with water. My skull was still throbbing. But my friend took me severely to task. 'You did it again. Once again you tried to abandon me!'

'You know I didn't have a choice.'

We held each other in our arms. I didn't ask Evin what had happened to her. Her tear-stained face and the bruise under her eye told me more than I wanted to know. Now she gave free rein to her tears. 'Farida, I've got bad news: Galib's planning to sell me,' she sobbed.

'What? How do you know?'

'He told me today. I think he was furious because I resisted.'

'I'm sure he was just trying to intimidate you,' I said. The idea of being separated from Evin was a nightmare for me. Amid all the horror we were experiencing, her presence afforded me some comfort at least – the last I had.

'I don't know,' she said. 'Perhaps you're right.'

We clutched at this hope. I think we both felt the same. We were ashamed to be seen by each other in such a miserable state, ashamed, too, that the other had witnessed things nobody should ever see (or at least that's what we thought at the time). On the other hand, we were the last tie for each other to our former world. The world in which she and I had been normal young women with a home and family. I was afraid of going mad if I lost Evin as well. Perhaps she feared the same thing – not for herself, but for me.

'I'll tell him I have to look after you,' she promised. 'I'll do everything he demands. If Galib possesses even a vestige of humanity he'll understand that I've got to stay with you.' But both of us had our doubts.

'If Zeyad tries it with me again, and you're taken away from me, I'm going to kill myself,' I told her.

'You can't!' she implored. 'You promised!'

'If you're not with me any more it doesn't matter, does it?'

'Even if I'm not with you, you must never give this man power over your life like that. No matter what he does. We'll find a way out of here. I promise you.'

But I wouldn't change my mind. 'I can't go on any more. Please understand me,' I begged her. 'We might not see each other again.'

Evin didn't say anything. But secretly I think she understood my motivation better than she was willing to admit.

At some point in the night we heard footsteps approaching our cell. We jumped. What did they want from us now? The lock rattled and the door opened. Galib entered, accompanied by an ISIS guard. Had they come to fetch Evin? I clung on tight to my friend. No, don't take her away, I thought in desperation. Having taken everything else from me, please leave me Evin at least!

'Get up!' Galib bellowed. At first it wasn't clear whether he meant Evin or both of us. Neither of us made a move to get to our feet. We stayed on our mattress and I held Evin even more tightly.

'Hey, I'm talking to you!' Galib took a step towards Evin and grabbed her. I started crying when he pulled her away from me.

'Evin!' I sobbed.

'Let me stay with her!' she begged. 'Farida needs me.'

Galib laughed. 'At this very moment there's someone else who needs you even more.'

He yanked her roughly towards the door. I refused to let go of her hand and tried to follow them. But Galib shoved me back into the room. 'No, you're staying there. The Emir will decide what's going to happen to you. And I can tell you now: he's absolutely furious at all your antics. So prepare for the worst!'

'My little sister is ill,' Evin said, making another attempt. 'Can't you see? She cannot be without me.'

'Don't tell fibs, girl,' Galib snapped at her. Grabbing Evin's arm, he wrenched her into the hallway while she still continued to resist.

'She's an epileptic. If I don't care for her she'll die!' she exclaimed.

'She doesn't die that easily. We've seen that already.'

The man with Galib locked the door behind the two of them. 'Evin!' I screamed, hammering wildly on the wood. Now I was alone in the cell. I heard the footsteps getting further away. Evin's protests grew quieter. Where were they taking her?

'Evin!' I kept crying when the men were long out of earshot. 'Evin! Evin!' I felt lonelier than I'd ever been in my life before. Now they'd taken away the last thing I had.

For a while I just sat there. Tears ran down my face. I'd hit rock bottom.

I felt as if someone had pulled a plug out of me and all the life that I'd once possessed had been released. There wasn't a spark of energy left in my body, nor of hope. Everything was lost. The only thing I wanted was to put an end to it all. I wanted to die. This time, however, the desire did not come from a desperation to escape some concrete threat. It was far too late for that anyway; everything had already happened. Now I just wanted my peace, I wanted to remove myself from the cruel world I'd fallen into. But how?

I looked down at myself. I was still shrouded in the black material I'd been wearing when Emir Zeyad carried me across the street and back into my prison. Otherwise there was nothing else in the room except for the two mattresses, the barred window and a pole with several clothes hooks fixed to the wall.

The material, the clothes hooks – could I use them to kill myself? The last time I'd tried, my veil had torn, ruining my plan. But I'd been in a hurry because I was afraid my 'owner' might come at any moment. This time I'd approach it with greater care.

So I took off the black cloak and started tearing it into strips. I tied these into a rope which seemed pretty solid. Once again I made a noose and tied it to the pole. This also appeared to be fairly solidly anchored in the wall. It just had to work, I thought. Enough was enough. I no longer wanted to be any part of this horror.

I put the noose around my neck. Unlike last time, however, there was no bed I could jump from. So I lifted my legs. I felt the noose tightening. I gasped. I felt dizzy. I don't know for sure what happened after that. I presume my legs fell back down to the floor and prevented me from strangling myself.

I was dangling there in a semi-conscious state, with my head in a noose. I kept trying to pull my legs up to accelerate the process of dying. But each time I lost consciousness and with it the capacity to maintain control over my limbs. Eventually the hook tore away from the wall and I crashed to the floor. I'd failed again.

Emir Zeyad came in the morning and found me crumpled on the floor of the cell. He flew into a rage. 'You miserable bitch!' he yelled. 'If you're that desperate to die maybe I can help you. I'm going to teach you a lesson!'

He threw me over his shoulder, taking the pole with the hooks too as he carried me from the cell. Strangely enough, it didn't seem to bother the Emir at all that I was totally uncovered and only wearing the hated blue dress he'd abused me in. He paid no attention to the fact that the other men saw me like this. On the contrary, he encouraged them to follow him. They didn't need a second invitation. I was taken to the room where Evin and I had been put when we arrived. Zeyad laid me across a table and got someone to fetch some electric cable. Then he flogged me as hard as he could.

'You devilish whore!' he berated me. 'Did you think I'd let you play games with me? I'll show you!'

He flogged my back until the blood started to flow beneath my blue dress. A group of about twenty men were standing watching. They were egging him on and accompanying his violent rage with cries of *Allahu akbar.* 'Go on, show her!' they shouted. 'Show her how we treat people who pray to Satan!'

Zeyad was beside himself. He kept thrashing me ever more wildly. Sometimes he used the cable, then the pole with the hooks he'd brought with him. He abused my entire body, not sparing my legs or head either. He whacked my face with the pole, injuring my left eye so I couldn't see out of it any more. I think he wanted to kill me, or at least he didn't care whether or not I survived. I still bear the scars today of his inconceivably brutal actions.

Eventually, when the pain became insufferable, I passed out.

*

When I slowly came round again I was back in my cell. I lay in a state of semi-consciousness, sensing that nobody had attended to my wounds. The blood on my back and the rest of my body had dried. Soon the wounds began to inflame and I felt feverish. After two days the guard gave me a little water, but nobody else bothered about me.

At first I was too weak even to go to the loo, something I'm ashamed to admit. But in my helplessness I had no other choice than to urinate in the cell I lay in, which only exacerbated the hygienic situation. I could barely stomach my own stench. Later I battered on the door and, watched by my guard, crept on all fours to the loo to relieve myself. If only I'd died, I kept thinking. How much longer did I have to put up with this torture? When would I finally be released from my ordeal?

Mostly I just lay there trying to cope with the pain. I thought a lot about my family, especially my favourite brother Delan. I saw the two of us racing in the car through the mountains, felt the sun on my face and the breeze blowing through the open window. What a lovely, carefree time we'd had together! We'd never realised how wonderful our life had been until it was suddenly wrenched away from us. I was terribly worried about him, and about Serhad and Dad too, who'd been driven off with him. Where had the men with the lorries taken them? Were they all right, or were they imprisoned like me? Had any of them even survived the day our village was attacked? I recalled with horror the shots that had echoed around the school building. If only I knew they were all right, everything here would be easier to bear.

On the other hand at least they couldn't see me in this pitiful state. If they knew how dreadful my current existence was they'd make themselves sick with worry and grief. And I'd almost die of shame in front of them.

I thought of Evin too. Where was my friend now? Would I ever see her again? How was life with her new 'owner'? Or had she perhaps found a way to escape? I deeply wished that to be the case, but didn't really believe it.

I don't know exactly how long I stayed in the cell in that appalling state. Whether it was a few days or a week – what difference did it make anyway? Time passed but it no longer had any significance for me. At one point I wondered if the Emir had forgotten me. But although I was feeling dreadful and in urgent need of medical attention, I was glad not to see my tormentor.

Eventually I learned that Zeyad had gone off again to fight somewhere else. Hopefully his opponents would get him this time, I thought angrily. I wished every ill in this world on that man. I really believe that if he stood before me today I wouldn't hesitate one second to kill him. It would only be fair and just in view of what he did to me.

Unfortunately, however, my sinister hopes proved unfounded. The Emir returned victorious. And, like the last time, I heard the *Allahu akbar* cries outside again. The men were celebrating their leader.

In my cell I grew nervous. Would Zeyad want to pleasure himself with a woman again after the battle? I couldn't for the life of me imagine that in my current state I could appear attractive to him. I was filthy, badly injured and barely able to move. And I wasn't able to put up a fight either.

Shortly afterwards I heard the footsteps of several men heading for my cell. I listened anxiously and full of terrible foreboding. Was the Emir among them? Would he try to rape me again? Terrified, I backed once more into a corner. But I knew I wouldn't be able to protect myself.

The lock rattled and the door opened. Emir Zeyad and two of his men stood before me, their legs apart. 'You're still here then, you stinking whore,' the ISIS commander said in a tone of boredom. 'But I can't look at you any more. Or smell you either.' He pointedly held his nose.

'Get her out of my sight!' he ordered the men.

7

IN THE MILITARY CAMP

On the Emir's orders the ISIS soldiers carried me out of my cell. I was in such a bad way I couldn't even struggle, let alone walk. The men made no effort to handle me as one ought to an injured person. They threw me roughly onto the back seat of a military vehicle. And to my horror they thanked the Emir. What for? I wondered warily.

We drove along bumpy roads towards the desert. I fleetingly thought of how Delan had taught me to drive. In my father's Opel Omega we'd simply head off into the mountains and, when we were out of sight, Delan would let me get behind the wheel. I loved turning the key and feeling the engine juddering into life. On the deserted tracks of Mount Sinjar I was allowed to drive as fast as I liked. Usually we never came across another soul on our trips. Delan and I set so many speed records, or at least we fancied we did.

But these outings with Delan seemed years ago now. Today I was strapped into a car driven by sinister-looking men, and I had no idea where we were going. Later, I picked up from what they were saying that we were heading for the 'Omar' gas field, and from the position of the golden sun standing above the horizon I calculated that it must be afternoon. Otherwise I had little orientation. I also thought that they might just chuck me out by the side of the road and leave me to die. But they had other plans for me.

The soldiers took me to an ISIS outpost near the gas field, a military camp which was essentially a collection of white living containers in the dust of the desert. As I later found out, around a hundred of Assad's soldiers used to be stationed here, then the rebels of the Free Syria Army. Finally ISIS had occupied the camp. It was right beside the gas field, which had been so keenly contested between the government and the rebels. The jihadis were trying to keep hold of this important resource.

Our vehicle stopped outside the container where the women of the camp were kept prisoner. It was in the centre of the camp, surrounded on all sides by soldiers' billets. I couldn't believe my eyes when I saw Evin come to the door. She was wearing a black veil. The reflection of the evening sun danced around her beautiful brown eyes. 'Farida?' she said when the men opened the rear door and she found me slumped in the back seat. I must have painted a shockingly sorry picture. 'Is it really you?'

'Evin,' I moaned.

We cried tears of joy at seeing each other again, something we hadn't reckoned on. My friend said something to the men and watched them carry me to the container, putting me down by the door. 'Be careful with her,' she urged them.

'She's a tough one this girl, she'll cope,' the men said. But they were wrong; I could barely move on my own. I had to crawl to make it to one of the mattresses. It was a great humiliation for me to have to move like that in front of the others. But I had no choice. Though deeply ashamed, I managed to smile at Evin and the six other girls she shared this space with.

'My God, Farida, what did he do to you?' Evin asked when she could see just how bad a shape I was in. She crouched down to take a closer look at my injuries, but I waved her away as if it wasn't that bad.

'He's an animal – you're well aware of that.'

She nodded. We didn't need to discuss it any further. 'But now you're here,' she said.

'Yes, I'm here.' I wasn't exactly sure what that meant. What happened in this camp? And what role did we girls play? When I asked Evin her reply was evasive.

'We help with the day-to-day chores,' she said.

'What else?'

'What do you mean, what else?'

Changing the subject, my friend introduced me to the other six Yazidis. Nase, Besma, Pervan, Sila, Sumeya and Reva were younger than us. They all slept on a pile of mattresses on the floor. None of them came from Kocho itself, but from the same area, which meant I was roughly able to work out which clan each of them belonged to, and whether we were distantly related. I immediately asked them if they had any news as to the whereabouts of our family members. But the girls had scant information. Like Evin and me, they'd spent most of the time imprisoned somewhere. One of them had heard that the older women and children from Kocho were still in Tal Afar. But they had no idea how they were being treated or what sort of conditions they were living in. Were my mum and brothers there too? And how were they? I was suddenly overcome by a wave of longing.

If I knew that they were still alive and all right, and that I'd see them again some day, I could cope with all this, I thought. How lovely it would be if my mum could make me fresh lemonade again and hide it in the fridge to stop me from swiping it prematurely with one of my friends, Evin or Nura. Just thinking about the drink, I fancied I could smell the aroma of the lemons from our garden, and my mouth started watering. How wonderful our life in Kocho had been! In retrospect, the time prior to the catastrophe seemed almost free from worry: our hours together in the garden, the prayers on the roof, the family excursions to Lalish. I knew that my life would never again be so carefree. But if I could recover even a fraction of what I'd lost, I was prepared to fight for it and stay alive.

'Don't lose heart, Farida,' Evin said. 'We'll find a way home.'

'Do you really believe that?' I sniffed.

'I'm absolutely certain. You've just got to get better again. Then we'll find a way out,' she promised, carefully stroking my forehead that Zeyad's blows had disfigured. 'Everything will be fine; you'll see. We're going to get through this together.'

Evin helped me into a small bathroom situated exactly in the middle of the two rooms that made up the container and which was accessible via doors on both sides. My friend washed the wounds on my head, legs and back. They were burning. 'We've got to get you to a doctor right away,' she said. Evin gave me some clean clothes: a skirt and blouse. Then she took me back into the room with the mattresses. To my astonishment I now noticed that there were even two windows, although they were covered by curtains.

As sunset was approaching, the girls stood in a row at the window. Knowing what they were about to do, I burst into tears. I tried in vain to stand up beside them, as was right and proper. My friends raised their hands in prayer. In my seated position I copied them. 'Amen, amen, amen,' we mumbled quietly so that no one outside could hear. 'May the Lord protect our religion. Our religion will survive.'

Now the muezzin was calling the ISIS soldiers to prayer too. The girls scattered. Soon afterwards a man banged on the door. 'Come on, it's time,' he commanded. Wrapping their black veils around their heads they followed him outside. Evin explained to the man that I was too weak to take part in the obligatory prayer. He glanced at me and nodded.

'But as soon as she's recovered she's joining in,' he said.

'Of course,' Evin assured him.

'Who does she belong to?'

Evin gave a very quiet answer, before scurrying out of the room with the other girls.

I crawled to the window and pushed the curtain slightly to one side. Using my arms I managed to pull myself up far enough to be able to peer outside. As I said, our container was in the middle of the camp, surrounded by other identical-looking ones. Between them was an empty space where around one hundred ISIS soldiers had now gathered. Many were wearing half-length beige tunics and cloth trousers. Like the other ISIS men I'd encountered up till now they all had beards, but only a few wore turbans. The fashion in this camp was for round prayer caps.

Kneeling on their prayer mats, the men carried out the Islamic rituals in sync. Behind them, and slightly to one side stood the group of girls, strictly covered in black veils. They too were praying in the Islamic fashion.

I didn't know what to think of this. Hadn't our fathers and grandfathers exhorted us in no uncertain terms never to betray our religion? On the other hand, with their secret prayer in the container the girls had just proven that our faith was still dear to their hearts. At any event, I was glad that I didn't have to stand out there with them. Not yet.

When Evin came back she didn't look me in the eye. And because I knew that it was upsetting for her I refrained from mentioning the prayer. 'What were you talking to that man about?' I asked her instead.

'Nothing,' she said. 'What do you mean?'

'You know exactly what I'm talking about.' I was, of course, referring to the man's question about who I 'belonged' to. Evin clearly knew more than she was letting on. 'How does it work here? Who is our "owner"?'

Evin lowered her gaze. She confessed to me that in fact every girl was the 'property' of someone at the base. The man who'd bought Evin was called Mahmudi, a middle-ranking commander. From the way Evin talked about him I knew she loathed the man. She didn't tell me what he did to her, and I didn't dare ask.

Instead I asked apprehensively, 'What about me? Who bought me?'

'No one bought you,' she said. 'The Emir gave you as a present.'

'To whom?'

'Azzad.' She told me that Azzad was one of the two men who'd come to fetch me. The young soldier had clearly distinguished himself in the battle for the gas field. Common foot soldiers in ISIS didn't usually get women, or only in recognition for special achievements. In spite of the grim state I was in, I was obviously a good enough gift for a man of his rank.

'I think he's all right,' Evin said. 'At least he's halfway friendly to us girls.'

I could barely imagine this to be true of an ISIS soldier, but I breathed a small sigh of relief. At least the man hadn't yet made any move to claim his rights as my 'owner', although that may have been related to the state of my health.

'However . . .' Evin said, pausing.

'What?'

She bit her lip. 'In actual fact he doesn't want you. He's already told me he's going to sell you.'

Things had already moved on by that evening. Azzad came into the container with a considerably older man, and I realised he was presenting me to his potential buyer. Amjed had white, almost transparent skin, shoulder-length hair and a long, light brown beard. He was slightly portly. As he was from Azerbaijan his Arabic was poor.

'Hey, girl, do you speak Arabic?' he asked. 'Do you understand me?'

As always I said nothing. 'My sister doesn't speak Arabic,' Evin said.

'Oh well, it's not so important.'

The men went and concluded the deal outside our container. I listened to the conversation. 'She doesn't look particularly agreeable at the moment,' Azzad said. 'But that will change when she's back to full health.'

'Why don't you keep her, then?' Amjed asked doubtfully.

'I can't afford the doctor's fees.'

'Does she really need urgent treatment?'

'Yes, otherwise she'll never get back on her feet again.'

The Azerbaijani seemed to think this over. 'Hmm . . .' he said, undecided.

'Listen, my friend,' Azzad said, 'I'll do you a special price of fifty dollars.'

'Really?' the Azerbaijani said in disbelief.

'If you promise you'll have a doctor look at her,' the young soldier said, setting his conditions.

'Deal,' Amjed agreed.

Through the curtain I saw them shake hands. So I was worth fifty dollars. The ISIS soldier had supplemented his pay and sorted out medical treatment for me, which he couldn't afford himself. So did he ultimately feel a hint of responsibility for me?

'Azzad's different from the others,' Evin said as if reading my thoughts. 'It's a shame you can't stay with him.'

'What's different about him?'

'He got involved with them through some silly chain of events. And now he regrets it. But he can't get away.'

'How do you know?'

'Because he told me when Mahmudi sent me to clean his container.' I presumed the girls were regularly given such tasks by their 'owners'. 'He said he felt sorry for us and in truth he was just as much a prisoner in the camp as we were.'

'Huh,' I said, unsure what to make of all this. It was easy to say such things. 'But there must have been a time when he supported ISIS. He wouldn't have joined them otherwise.'

'He says they brainwashed him.'

As I continued to puzzle over Azzad's behaviour, Amjed sent a doctor to examine me. Amjed came in as well to oversee things. As my new 'owner' he didn't want to take any risks by leaving me with another man, even if it was a doctor. ISIS soldiers didn't do such things. They knew each other too well, and when it came to women they didn't trust anyone else an inch.

But in fact the doctor wasn't an ISIS man; you could tell that at first glance. He didn't have a beard, nor did he wear anything on his cropped hair. His clothes, too, were those of a civilian. That's why I liked him. The doctor gave me a thorough examination, especially my back, pelvis, legs and the injury to my head. Evin also told him about my epileptic fits. He looked extremely concerned. 'She's in a very poor condition,' he told Amjed.

'What does that mean?'

'She needs peace and quiet, complete rest.'

'For how long.'

'She should stay in bed for at least ten days.'

I saw Amjed's face change to register the disappointment.

'I'll give her an infusion and something for the pain.'

But the Azerbaijani wasn't listening any more; he only had one thing on his mind. 'Doctor, how long will it be before she's functioning properly again?' he asked impatiently.

'I can't say yet. For the moment, at least, no one must touch her.' I rejoiced inside. That's what you get, you old lech, I thought. What a bad investment your fifty dollars were!

I rapidly became familiar with the routines in the camp, even though to begin with I spent all my time in bed in the container. They revolved around a few fixed things, including the prayer times, which everyone in the camp had to observe, whether willingly or forced. Five times a day the entire camp, including the abducted women, assembled in the empty space between the containers.

'Why don't you refuse?' I asked Evin.

'I tried at first,' she said. 'But they beat me to a pulp. They don't mess around. It doesn't mean anything, Farida, believe me.'

And I did. For every morning and evening, before or after the men came to fetch them, the girls secretly celebrated their own ritual. All the same it made me cross that my friends pretended to pray to the same god as our enemies. I was angry at our helplessness and I resolved not to join in under any circumstances.

The second thing determining the daily routine of the girls was the men's needs. Evin and the others were repeatedly summoned by their 'owners'. Officially this meant that they had to perform housework. Sometimes this was actually the case and they would scrub their masters' containers or do their washing.

Cooking was not one of their chores, because the men were fed from a central canteen. A cook, usually Azzad, prepared them Libyan-style food, meaning that everything was mixed together on the same plate: rice, vegetables, fish and salad. Azzad would bring us a plate, too, which we all ate from together with forks. Although we didn't like the food much, we were always starving and very grateful to Azzad for thinking of us at least. The other soldiers seemed to forget that we needed to eat too.

But usually when the girls were summoned to the containers it was to perform another sort of service. My fellow prisoners didn't talk about it openly. But I could see them getting agitated and frightened whenever they were called. They would leave with their heads bowed in shame, and return with puffy faces. I soon figured out what this all meant, and it made me very afraid. Our slavery was first and foremost a sexual one. My friends were also taking the pill. They claimed that their 'owners' had prescribed this medicine for them and that they weren't sure what it was. But they could read and understand the writing on the packaging as well as I could.

When Evin came back from Mahmudi and took off her black veil, she regularly had scratches and marks on her body. She'd sit cross-legged beside me on the mattress, lay her head on my chest and start to cry softly, while I stroked her hair. We didn't have to talk about what had happened; I could tell that Mahmudi hurt my friend badly.

'Don't blame yourself,' I told her, for I knew that this is what tormented her most. We'd all been brought up to blame ourselves. But at least as far as my friends were concerned I could see that was wrong. 'There's nothing you can do about it.'

'But I feel so dirty!' she sobbed.

'Your soul is pure. He's the dirty one.'

'He's a pig, a brutal, lewd pig!'

'They're all pigs. They have no morality. And one day they'll get their just deserts. I'll make sure of that myself,' I swore, and meant it too.

My 'owner', Amjed, did leave me in peace to begin with. But the doctor came every day to check on me. He changed my infusion, treated my wounds and kept Amjed at arm's length. For that I was deeply grateful to the doctor and we soon became friends.

One time, when we were alone, he admitted to us that he was truly sorry about our plight, and ashamed at what was being done in the name of his religion. 'I wish I could help you,' he said.

I recognised that he was a good man. My brain whirred into action. 'Buy me then,' I suggested. Forgetting all caution, I even spoke to him in Arabic. 'And then let me escape, me and Evin.'

But he only shook his head sadly. 'I wish that were possible,' he said. 'But I can't buy you; I don't have the right.'

'Why not?'

He sighed, then revealed his secret. 'I don't belong to them,' he said, explaining that ISIS had kidnapped him in the hospital when they took Deir ez-Zor. 'We're in the same boat,' he said. 'I'm just as much a prisoner as you are. That's why I can't help you.'

I understood what he was saying, but refused to accept it. 'Please think whether there's anything you can do for us,' I encouraged him. 'Your God will reward you for it.'

'But that's what I'm doing, that's what I'm doing.'

When my condition hadn't significantly improved after ten days, the doctor told Amjed that he had to take me to hospital. Only there could I be properly examined. The Azerbaijani objected. 'Is that really necessary, doctor?'

'If you want her to be able to walk again, there's no way round it.'

Reluctantly Amjed agreed. Clearly, what he was most annoyed about was having to pay for the treatment. But that had been his deal with Azzad, so he couldn't shirk his responsibility. But I think he was already regretting having gone into the deal without thinking.

'I really got a dud with you, didn't I, girl? You're causing me nothing but problems!' he cursed.

'Tell him that I'm not happy being with him either,' I said to Evin, who was as usual acting as my translator, because I supposedly didn't speak a word of Arabic. He went into a rage.

'Tell her to keep her trap shut!' he barked at us. 'She's given me enough grief already!'

In our region it's very rare to go to hospital alone, and this hadn't changed under ISIS control. Evin was desperate to accompany me, but Mahmudi wouldn't let her. Maybe he was worried that the two of us would escape together. Sumeya, a shy sixteen-year-old, came with me instead. After the two of us had covered ourselves in black from head to toe, Amjed packed us into a car he'd borrowed from somebody and drove us to Mayadin hospital in Deir ez-Zor.

The hospital was very close to the airport, where there was constant fighting. As soon as we got out of the car we could hear firing in the distance: rifle shots, but also the thunder of artillery. If only ISIS's opponents would take the hospital, I wished secretly as Amjed carried me into the building on his shoulders.

The facility was still in the hands of the military; armed guards stood around the entrance. Inside things were running fairly normally, though there was a strict separation of the sexes. Amjed explained to the staff that the room Sumeya and I stayed in must be locked from the outside at all times. This was agreed to without question; Amjed's status as a fighter allowed him to issue such orders. We were in the middle of a war after all.

After he'd left me and my escort alone, the doctors carried out all sorts of tests on me. They X-rayed my back and legs to check for fractures that might have been overlooked till now. To examine my head they inserted me into a long tube, a diagnostic technique they called MRI. I think this had been ordered by the camp doctor, because since Zeyad's beatings I'd had constant headaches and dizziness, as well as two recent epileptic attacks at night.

I recall little of my time in hospital, as I was given fairly strong painkillers – morphine, I think. For most of it I was only semi-conscious. Having my body numbed in this way was a very pleasant experience; it gave me respite from the permanent pain I'd had to endure since my abuse at the hands of the Emir. I'd have been very happy to keep on taking the drugs.

I don't know what emerged from the tests; they didn't share the findings with me. Nor do I know whether further therapy or an operation was necessary. The doctors didn't talk to me. They only revealed to my 'owner' what they'd discovered about me. Whether it was out of fear, conviction or opportunism, the entire staff at the clinic behaved loyally towards the ISIS leadership.

I was quite disappointed when after three days Amjed packed me into the car and took me back to the camp. For some reason I'd imagined that it wouldn't come to this as the hospital would be taken by ISIS's opponents beforehand. I'd been hoping for a miracle, but it didn't happen.

When the Azerbaijani showed the camp doctor my X-rays and MRI scans, the man put his head in his hands and asked why on earth he hadn't left me in the hospital. The answer was simple: Amjed would have had to pay for any further treatment, and clearly this exceeded by far the budget for his 'slave'. All the doctor could do was give the strict order that I needed more time in bed.

It was only after a month and a half inside the camp, which I spent mainly in bed in the container, that I recovered somewhat. By now autumn had arrived, the sun shone less powerfully and its rays had given way to a softer light. At this stage I could even manage the few steps to the door to enjoy its warmth. I was careful, however, not to overdo it; I didn't want to harm my status as an 'invalid'. For I was still excused from all obligations, of which the communal prayer was only one. I often wondered uneasily how much longer I'd manage to keep it like this.

This was also the usual time of our autumn congregation in Lalish. In our imprisonment we wistfully remembered how we'd spent these days in the past. It was in Lalish, we Yazidis believed, that God once came down to earth. Here He created the Seven Angels, the sun, the moon and the stars, all flora and fauna, the rivers and the seas. Everything, therefore, began in Lalish a long time ago. Human beings too were created in this place of earthly perfection. Back then, each September we would visit Lalish, where under the leadership of the Peacock there was a meeting of the Seven Angels who control destiny on earth. They would discuss the events of the coming year and make important decisions about the future of humanity. We went to Lalish to accompany the angels as they held their discussions and to beg for leniency. I recalled the delight my brothers and I felt when my father told the old stories on our way to the shrine. Would there ever be a return to normality for us? Did Lalish even still exist? What remained of the world we once knew? Did the Seven Angels continue to meet even if we couldn't accompany them with our rituals and songs? They had not wished well for us last year. What would they decide for the year to come?

Amjed, who paid regular visits to our container to see whether I was making progress, grew increasingly impatient. 'How much longer now, doctor?' he'd keep asking. And each time he'd be put off. In the end his patience snapped. He was desperate finally to enjoy his 'property'.

'You've been fine for a while now, Farida,' he exploded on one of his visits. 'I've waited long enough. You're going to come with me to my container right now.'

I froze and stayed lying there as stiff as a poker, pretending not to have understood a word he'd said.

'Enough of the games,' he warned me. 'You understand me perfectly well. And you know that I've got a right to you. I've invested a lot of money in you!'

I remained silent again.

'All right. Either you come now of your own accord, or I'll have you fetched.'

He left. Shortly afterwards, two low-ranking ISIS soldiers came to our container. They grabbed me roughly under my arms. I kicked and screamed as they took me to the door, but they were unfazed. Accompanied by the lewd gaze and whistling of other ISIS men, who stopped outside our container, they dragged me right across the camp to Amjed's billet. Shoving me inside, they slammed the door behind me.

The Azerbaijani was already waiting for me. I don't think I ever found that man quite as repulsive as at that moment when I saw him sitting smugly, his legs apart, on one of the two wide beds in the small room. He was dressed in the uniform beige tunic and trousers. He'd already taken off his army boots and the cap he always wore on his head. I stood rooted to the spot by the door.

'I've waited long enough,' he said. 'God is my witness that this is so. I have a right to you!'

He rolled out his mat and got ready to kneel down and pray. I'd heard from my friends that the particularly religious ones commonly did this before taking a woman, thereby celebrating their rape as a form of worship.

In this moment when his attention was diverted, I tried to yank open the window. Although still not fully fit, I thought I might be able to save myself by leaping out. But Amjed realised what I had in mind and grabbed me from behind. 'Little bitch!' he spat. 'For months you play the invalid and now you want to try some acrobatic tricks. I'll show you!'

He held me tight and cut down his prayer to a few surahs from the Quran, which he muttered in a hurry. Then he was ready. He ripped off my clothes. I resisted wildly. 'You will obey me!' Amjed cried, pulling down my veil. I screamed blue murder. He threw me onto the bed. I desperately looked for a way to escape his control. But he pressed me down. Despite his age he was stronger than I'd thought.

I tried biting his arm. But nothing helped. I could not prevent Amjed from doing what he'd planned. When he finally got off me, I curled up into a ball and stayed on the bed, crying.

Amjed pulled up his trousers, put his cap back on and stomped out of the room in his army boots.

I had an attack that same night. It developed from a dream in which Amjed pointed his fat, fleshy fingers at me. These fingers had soon grown huge and surrounded me on all sides. I felt unable to breathe. In my dream – but in real life too – the very familiar twitching and jerking began. My racket must have woken the other girls and Evin, who lay beside me. But I have no recollection of this.

When I came to, the light in the container was on and all the girls were standing around me. There was a look of horror on their faces. Evin was holding my torso tightly and pressing me onto the mattress. 'Farida!' she called out. 'Can you hear me? Please wake up, Farida!'

'Yes,' I replied weakly. Evin stroked my face. The sight of my friend comforted me a little. I soon realised what had happened.

'Everything's all right,' Evin said to me. 'You mustn't worry.'

'Yes, Evin,' I said just to be polite.

'It's all over now,' she reassured me. 'Come on, let's go back to sleep. You'll have forgotten everything by the morning.'

I started to cry. No, there was one thing I knew I'd never forget. If I ever regained my freedom, I'd scream out this injustice to the whole world.

Subsequently Amjed forced me into his container on a number of occasions. Each time I fought with him: I screamed, bit him, thrashed around and used all my strength to spoil his fun. I had no desire to be an easy victim; I wanted him to tire himself out and lose the urge before it happened. But in the end he always got the upper hand because he was physically stronger. He had no regard any longer for the state of my health, which continued to be precarious.

Each time he would carry out his religious ritual beforehand. This I found especially repellent. How could these oh-so-pious people so shamefacedly pass the responsibility for their sordid acts onto their God? These people believed hell existed, so did they harbour no concerns about being dragged down there and called to account? I couldn't understand how they could view what they did as their religious right. Couldn't they see that by making such claims they were lying to themselves first and foremost? Their behaviour was not in the least God-fearing; it was inhumane, and a disgrace to their religion which they thereby dishonoured.

Now that I was regarded as 'healthy' again, the men also forced me to take part in the daily prayers. I resisted, of course. The first morning they requested me to join, I got Evin to tell them that the doctor had forbidden me to carry out the movements, because I had to protect my back.

'You say to her that if she doesn't stop telling lies, we'll chivvy her along,' came their aggressive reply. 'When she's healthy it's her owner who decides what happens, not the doctor.' Before Evin could finish translating they had already grabbed my arms and were lugging me outside. 'Get up!' they ordered. 'Pray!'

'Tell them I can't,' I said to Evin, as I sat motionless on the prayer mat. Soon they started hitting me with the butts of their rifles.

'If you don't start showing respect for the one true God, we'll see to it that you really won't be able to get up.'

'Tell them that their God will be ashamed of them,' I told Evin, painstakingly intimating a genuflection so that they would finally leave me in peace. 'Tell them they're committing a great sin and that they'll burn in hell for it!'

These altercations were almost a daily occurrence. I and the other girls too did our best to provoke the men when we were forced to pray. Sometimes we recited the surahs wrongly, or we'd only make half-hearted attempts at the movements. But we always ensured that these displays of resistance were as subtle as possible, for open refusal to pray was punished severely. Once I was even shot at by a soldier, because supposedly I hadn't been praying correctly. In truth, however, I'm sure he deliberately aimed away from my body; he was just out to terrify me. But I tried not to let it intimidate me. When in doubt I was always ready to pay the price for my reticence.

On another occasion I managed to convince the girls to turn up to prayer unveiled. Alarmed, the pious men covered their eyes with their hands when we stepped out of the container. Some, especially the younger men among them, took the ISIS ideology very seriously. They really believed they'd joined a God-fearing outfit and were fighting for a just cause. As they regarded Islam – or their interpretation of it – as a panacea, they thought it capable of solving all problems. These young boys were utterly naive and blinded. Even when they beat us after such shows of defiance, so we wouldn't dare repeat them, they believed they were serving their God and doing good. When will they finally wake up? I wondered.

They were very serious about trying to make us convert to Islam, which is why they weren't just content to force their prayers on us. They took great pains to turn us into Muslim women, giving us religious education twice a week. This basically consisted of two bearded men coming into the container to read the Quran with us. They claimed to be imams. But as far as I know they weren't real clerics with proper training, just self-appointed Quran specialists. Evin, who spoke the best Arabic among us, had to translate for these 'teachers', and soon earned the nickname 'imam' from us.

Once during a lesson we were interrogated. One of the guards must have caught us turning to the sun on the steps of our container and told the teachers about it. 'Did you pray to the sun?' they asked us severely.

'Not at all,' Evin affirmed without hesitation.

But I saw it as a challenge. Surely this was the perfect opportunity to engage in a debate with our tormentors. Their objective was to proselytise us; mine was to sow doubt in their minds about whether they really knew their religion, by confronting them with the same religious texts they were serving up to us.

'Your religion does not permit you to impose your faith on us,' I told them through Evin, as we were still pretending that I didn't understand their language. 'The second surah says: "There shall be no compulsion in the religion." Are we supposed to learn this by heart but ignore its meaning? What kind of bizarre piety is that?'

The men seemed slightly rattled. Evin backed me up, citing another place in their holy book. Right at the end, in the 109th surah, it says, 'For you is your religion and for me is my religion.' Pointing to the sentence she said, 'Here it is in black and white! What gives you the right to assume your religion is the only true one when your prophet says otherwise?'

'There's something you haven't understood,' the men said. 'Here the prophet is referring to other religions with holy scriptures; so long as they pay the head tax Jews and Christians enjoy our protection. But you don't. You are idolaters, devil worshippers even.'

'No, we're not!'

'Be quiet, girl. What do you lot understand of Islam?' This is how it always went. Whenever they were at a loss they'd insult us, say we were 'infidels' and forbid us to talk because they'd run out of arguments.

Sometimes we'd have a go at them personally. 'Why did you desert your families?' we said provocatively. 'Why did you go to war to kill people? Doesn't your religion command that you look after your fathers and mothers?'

'Our parents weren't proper Muslims, so we had to leave them,' they responded, and probably meant it too. 'We're fighting for a caliphate in which justice will prevail and everyone will live according to God's laws.'

'They're not God's laws, they're not even the laws of Islam. You've made them up!'

'Quiet!' they shouted, threatening us with the cane, their secret educational weapon. 'By next time you'll have learned the ten verses of the second surah by heart. All of them, do you understand? Woe betide anyone who can't recite them.'

This was always our 'homework'. We had to learn by heart the sections of text we'd read together. At the next session the teachers would test us, caning anyone who couldn't recite the verses. Usually everyone was beaten, because none of us had any desire to adopt their faith. Given all that we'd had to endure, that really was asking too much.

But the ISIS men were genuine fanatics; they actually believed that they could summon magical powers just by uttering the surahs, somehow mysteriously drawing us over to their side. Oh, how wrong they were! With everything they tried to funnel into our minds, they were merely fuelling our rejection and contempt.

From week to week the instruction became more onerous, and we were permanently threatened with the cane. 'You're so stupid it's exasperating,' they bellowed. 'Your heads are empty!'

One of them took things too far. As he told us, his motive was personal. The man had accidentally run over two Muslims in his car, and in a fit of repentance he'd promised his God that he'd compensate for the deaths by creating two new Muslims. And so two of us girls were to learn the entire Quran by heart. He was particularly set on twelve-year-old Besma as he considered her the most malleable on account of her tender age. He'd administer an especially violent beating if she failed to learn anything.

The only time we had any peace in the camp was when the men were caught up in battle. They'd lock us in our container and leave us in the camp, deserted save for a handful of guards. We'd breathe a sigh of relief: no prayers, no forced visits to other containers, no beatings, no indoctrination.

On the other hand there was nothing to eat during these periods either, which often lasted several days. When Azzad, the young man I'd first belonged to, wasn't in the camp, nobody thought of providing for us. We would have to drink the dirty tap water and also use it to soften the dried slices of bread we'd collected and kept for such an eventuality. The door remained locked until our 'owners' returned and demanded our company once more.

*

Although each of us belonged to one man, this could change over time. If he became tired of his girl, didn't like her any more or she'd started to bore him, he'd sell her to another ISIS soldier.

Evin was one of the first this happened to. One day Mahmudi came to our container and told her that she was now the property of his friend Abu Muzaffar. Mahmudi had been an extremely brutal individual, who had beaten her regularly because it excited him sexually, so Evin wasn't sad to be rid of him. But when she heard that her new 'owner' was already waiting outside to enjoy her, she was shocked. Her face was ashen when the guards took her outside. At that moment I felt deeply sorry for my friend.

And yet I was pleased that Mahmudi had 'only' sold her to another man in the camp, as at least it meant she would stay with me. I knew that without Evin I would go mad here.

Besma, too, soon found out that her 'owner' had changed. The Libyan Jamal had sold her to a compatriot. 'Go to Fahed,' Jamal told her. 'You belong to him now.'

But she refused. 'I don't belong to him and I never belonged to you either,' she protested bravely. 'You've got no right to sell me.'

'Oh really?' he said, amused. He offered her his rifle. 'Take it. Kill yourself if you don't want to go to him.'

Besma took the gun and chucked it on the floor. She knew he was just teasing her and that the gun wasn't loaded, which is why she didn't bother trying to use it. In any case, our desire to take our own lives had passed by this stage. The worst thing they could do to us had already occurred long ago. There was only one thing we wanted now: to survive this nightmare and bear witness. 'Why should I do that? Kill yourself instead!' Besma said.

'Goodness me! I've never seen you so feisty!' Jamal laughed. Then he beat her until she was lying on the floor, groaning in pain. Besma still had to go to Fahed afterwards.

One day Amjed told me that he was leaving the camp to go and fight with another ISIS unit in Raqqa. It was obvious that he felt like a stranger among all the Libyans here. At first I thought I'd be rid of him, and was already secretly celebrating. But then it dawned on me that, as his 'property', of course I'd be moving with him. 'No!' I screamed, kneeling before him.

Through Evin, who continued to act as my 'translator', I let him know that I couldn't under any circumstances go without her. 'You know better than all the others that my sister is seriously ill,' Evin implored him. 'Please let me stay with her. Farida won't survive without me.'

'I'm not that keen on taking her anyway,' Amjed said bad-temperedly. 'This girl is really no fun at all – she'd just be a millstone round my neck.'

'Then ask around the camp to see if someone wants to buy her,' Evin suggested. Although supposedly I didn't understand a word of Arabic, I gave my friend an angry look when she said this. But then I realised that Evin's strategy made sense. In the logic of these men there were only two possibilities for us to stay together: either Amjed bought Evin – which I considered most unlikely as he wasn't a particularly rich man and, in any case, he'd had quite enough with me – or he found someone else in the camp to buy me. I was nauseated by the idea of having to put up with another man, irrespective of who he was. But in principle Amjed seemed to find Evin's suggestion a good one.

'No one's going to want this girl,' he moaned, 'because she's such a bloody cheeky devil. My God, I really ought to have got rid of her long ago.'

I couldn't help smiling to myself. Aha, I thought. My struggles and constant attempts at resistance were not completely ineffectual. I'd succeeded in spoiling Amjed's fun. And it also seemed that word had got round among the others that they wouldn't have an easy time with me. In view of all the hardship we'd had to bear, this at least was a minor victory.

'You might find someone interested in Farida,' my friend said, looking so mischievous that I was confused. What was she up to?

'I've got an idea,' Evin whispered to me when Amjed had left.

'What?'

'We'll ask Azzad to buy you.'

'Azzad?' I looked at Evin in astonishment. She was talking about my former 'owner', the nice young man who brought us food. The same man who said he regretted having joined ISIS and who, when I arrived in the camp, couldn't wait to sell me on, which we'd always interpreted as moral fibre. But perhaps it had just been awkwardness. Could we convince him to save me?

'I'll put it to him,' Evin said. 'I mean, we've got nothing to lose.'

She was right. Given the alternative of going with Amjed to Raqqa and leaving Evin behind, we could leave no stone unturned. We couldn't allow them to separate us again. I knew that without Evin's maternal care I wouldn't survive imprisonment, neither physically nor mentally. No, I couldn't be without her. On the other hand, I couldn't imagine Azzad going with her suggestion. After all, he didn't want a slave, and he'd already passed me on once before, virtually for nothing.

'Wouldn't it be better to try running away?' I asked her. By now I was able to walk again, although I couldn't move quickly, and I still had a pronounced limp. What was more, our prison, as I've already mentioned, was in the middle of the military camp, surrounded on all sides by containers in which the soldiers lived. The camp itself was protected by an outer ring of guards. So it certainly wouldn't be easy.

However, I'd recently exploited my purported inability to understand Arabic and listened in to a conversation among the soldiers. Some of them had evidently been approached by people smugglers asking about the girls in the camp. From what they said I inferred that they were toying with the idea of supplementing their pay by giving information. Naturally this was exciting news for us girls. Were our relatives using this method to look for us? Perhaps some of the men would prove open to bribery.

'We'll run away as soon as the opportunity presents itself,' Evin promised. 'But first of all we've got to buy some time.'

I looked at her doubtfully.

'If Azzad says no, we can always try to escape,' she conceded.

We didn't know for sure when Amjed was planning to leave, so we had no time to lose. The next time Azzad stood outside our door with a plate of steaming rice, Evin quickly pulled him into the container. The young Syrian was rather taken by surprise, for men who weren't our 'owners' weren't actually allowed inside the container.

'What's wrong?' he asked, bemused.

'You've always been good to us, Azzad,' Evin said, and I saw him blush at her words. This made me happy; although he was a soldier, Azzad had clearly not lost all of his humanity. 'Now we need your help.'

Azzad frowned. Maybe he was worried that we'd ask him to help us escape. That would be terribly risky for him; I knew he couldn't agree to it. 'What can I do for you?' he asked cautiously.

'You've got to buy Farida back,' Evin said. 'Otherwise Amjed will take her with him to Raqqa. Even though he hates her, she is still his property.'

Now Azzad stared at us in disbelief. 'Does Amjed know of your plan?' he asked.

'No, but I think he'd be open to it,' Evin said.

Azzad turned to me and I lowered my gaze in shame.

'I'll think about it,' he promised.

'Please don't take too long.'

Evin's plan actually worked. A few days later, a contented Amjed let me know that he was rid of me. Azzad had taken me back, he said. I've no idea what sort of financial arrangement the men came to, but I gave a sigh of relief; Azzad really was a good man, I thought. Perhaps everything would be different from now. Perhaps he would even help us escape.

Soon afterwards Azzad called for me, something he'd never done before. Two of his comrades came to fetch me. I had a strange feeling as they accompanied me to his container. There Azzad was sitting on his bed, his rifle close at hand. He didn't beat around the bush; he was one of the few who knew I spoke excellent Arabic.

'Farida, I want to take you as my wife,' he said.

I couldn't believe what I was hearing. I'd briefly regarded this man as my saviour, but the spell had quickly been broken. How could I have been so stupid and so wrong about him? In an instant, I realised that Azzad had only spurned me when I arrived in the camp because I was in such an appalling state. Now that I was better again, he saw things differently. He wasn't one iota better than the other ISIS men; he wanted to have sex with me. And like the others he, too, was quite happy to use his rifle to claim his supposed right.

I spat at him.

'If you hurt me I'll kill you,' I said slowly and in all seriousness.

'Farida,' he said, 'it's not what you think. I'll marry you.'

'But *I* won't marry *you*! Do you understand? I'm not going to marry any of you pigs! I don't belong to you!'

I rushed for the weapon beside him. It was a sudden impulse that drove me. Azzad was completely taken by surprise and so couldn't react quickly enough. I already had the rifle aimed at him. Because my father had shown me how to handle a gun I had it ready in a flash.

Azzad was shocked. 'Don't be silly, Farida,' he said. 'It's not loaded anyway.' He came up to me, seemingly unconcerned that I might pull the trigger.

'Stay exactly where you are or I'll shoot,' I hissed. He froze. So the rifle *was* loaded. I sensed a power that I hadn't felt in a long time: the certainty of being in control of my situation.

'Farida . . .' Azzad said quietly. 'I just wanted to . . . It's not what you think –'

'Oh yes, it's exactly what I think. But you can't just buy me. And you can forget right now the idea that I'm going to become your wife!'

'I don't want to force you to do anything,' he said. I didn't believe a word he said. With his protestations Azzad was just trying to break my concentration and take the weapon off me. But he wouldn't succeed. Before that happened I'd kill him and the entire camp, I swore. I'd use every bullet in the magazine.

'Abdul Hamid!' I heard him shout all of a sudden. This was the name of Azzad's neighbour, who lived in the room next door. The door opened and another ISIS man rushed in.

'What's happening?' he cried.

I aimed the gun at him. 'This is happening!'

'She's mad!' Azzad said. 'We've got to get the weapon off her!'

The two of them advanced from either side, which meant I no longer knew where to aim. Finally Abdul Hamid succeeded in wresting the rifle from me. Azzad tried to push me to the floor. But I knew his weak spot; he'd recently sustained a midriff injury in battle. I punched the wound as hard as I could. Azzad howled in pain.

'You're out of your mind,' he yelled in fury. 'You're going to pay for that!'

The two of them then managed to get me to the floor and hold me tight. 'You're a loose cannon, Farida,' Azzad said, gasping for breath.

'If all the Yazidi men had fought like you, I bet we wouldn't have defeated them,' Abdul Hamid said, amused.

'You didn't defeat us,' I corrected him. 'You took away our weapons and lured us into a trap. That was terribly cowardly of you.'

'Are you still so insolent?' Abdul Hamid said, threatening to beat me. But I knew that only my 'owner' had the right to do this, so I ignored him altogether. I sensed that Azzad wanted to send the other man away. The weakness he'd shown – dealing with a woman – was deeply embarrassing for him. But it wasn't so easy for him, particularly as I'd hurt him badly.

'Will you be all right with her?' Abdul Hamid asked.

'Of course,' Azzad said, grimacing with pain.

'How about your wounds?'

Azzad didn't reply. His mate understood. 'I'll call the doctor.'

'Farida, you've profoundly humiliated me. Why?' Azzad asked when we were alone. 'Do you want me to sell you again? I'll find the nastiest soldier in the whole camp, mark my words!'

Azzad was very angry. But I was surprised at him. Did he really think I wouldn't offer any resistance if he tried to force me to do something against my will?

'I don't belong to you or to any other man,' I repeated. 'I'll never belong to any of you, no matter what you do to me.'

'Don't you understand that the rules here are different from the world outside? You can't change them. You'll be punished for what you did just now – I'll make sure of that.'

'So what?' I said. 'I'll never abide by your rules. And if there's the slightest trace of honour left in your body, then you shouldn't either, Azzad.'

He said nothing. I realised that he didn't have the energy to argue back. And this pleased me. Perhaps I'd succeeded in planting a hint of doubt in his ISIS brain. Perhaps this seed would germinate one day.

The doctor arrived soon afterwards, and was amazed to see the damage I'd done. 'That looks very nasty,' he said to Azzad. 'Did the girl really do that?'

'Yes,' he said. 'But she's no normal girl. She's at least as strong as a man.'

Azzad gave the order for me to be taken back to the container. The camp chief would decide my punishment later. Despite this I secretly felt a sense of triumph when the ISIS soldiers took me away. I'd well and truly messed up Azzad's desire for a tryst, for now at least.

My friends treated me like a heroine when I told them about my struggle. 'You did brilliantly, Farida,' they cheered. Evin tapped me on the shoulder. 'Azzad won't be trying that again!'

I expressed my agreement, although I doubted she was right. 'We must offer more resistance,' I said. 'We've got to make life as difficult as possible for them. You can see it's worth it.'

'Maybe it'll mean they finally lose interest in us,' Besma said hopefully.

'We can definitely spoil their fun at any rate.'

All of us were in high spirits. My resistance seemed to have released unsuspected reserves of energy in my fellow prisoners. Besma showed us a pair of scissors she'd found while cleaning her 'owner's' container. 'The next time he tries it on with me I'm going to kill him,' she declared.

The others looked at her wide-eyed. 'You'd really dare do that? Just be careful,' said Reva, who was always a little more timid than the rest of us.

She and Sumeya had made a big mistake. They thought they might be able to tease some news out of the ISIS men about where their families were, so they'd given the soldiers the names of their mothers and siblings. As our enemies were now armed with this information, the two girls were vulnerable to blackmail and so less inclined to create trouble for our captors than the rest of us.

But Evin was worried about Besma too. After all, she was still a child in so many ways. 'I don't know if that's a good idea,' she warned. 'The men are very strong, you know.'

But she couldn't dissuade the girl from her plan. 'I'm stronger than he is,' Besma said. 'I'm going to kill him, you'll see.'

'Or he'll kill you.'

'I don't care.'

Evin and I looked at each other, unsure what to say. We understood that Besma had to try. Even if she didn't survive, at least she'd be saving her soul.

Which is why I said, 'I'll be very proud of you. And I'm absolutely certain you'll succeed.'

8

THE ROAD OUT OF HELL

When they brought Besma back to our container, her 'owner' had beaten her to within an inch of her life. Her face was red and swollen, while her back, bottom and legs bore the bloody weals of the belt he'd thrashed her with. My little friend was crying. In spite of this I had every reason to be proud of her. With her scissors Besma had actually tried to stab the man's heart while he was raping her. 'I did it,' she muttered beneath the tears as we attended to her wounds. 'It almost worked.'

I stroked her hair and comforted her. 'Poor little Besma,' I said. 'You're a heroine. Melek Taus will reward you for what you had the nerve to do. You're a brave woman.'

She snivelled and smiled. 'I'll try it again,' she said.

'You've got to get better first, little heroine.' I held her hand and waited for her to fall asleep, exhausted from her exertions and horrific experience.

'We've got to get out of here,' I told Evin and the others.

'You're telling me, Farida. If there were the slightest opportunity we wouldn't be here any more.'

'We've got to create the opportunity ourselves,' I said. I was thinking about my own situation. I knew it was only a matter of time before Azzad recovered and took revenge on me. What I dreaded far more than any beatings was the rape which inevitably awaited me. Incited by his mates, Azzad would try to claim what he considered to be his right. However diffident and kind he'd come across as in the past, this man was now my enemy because I'd offended his honour. Although he'd assigned a colleague to bring us things to eat from time to time, to prevent us from starving, he would pay me back for my impertinence.

I thought about this as we cleaned the containers. By now we were cleaning the entire camp. Our 'owners' would send us in groups of three to look after the containers of all their friends and colleagues. As I mopped the floor with Evin and Sumeya, I could see that the soldier whose billet we were working on must have just returned from battle. His field backpack was standing in one corner of the room. I had an idea.

'Let's search his backpack,' I said to my friends. 'Maybe we'll find something we can use.'

'I'd rather not,' Sumeya said. 'If anyone catches us we'll be for it.'

'Oh, come on, what can happen?' As I've said, my fear of physical punishment had long vanished. 'All they'll do is give us another beating!'

Evin, too, thought we should give it a try. We asked Sumeya to keep watch for us at the door. 'If we're caught you can still say you weren't part of it,' I reassured her.

She agreed. Sumeya stood by the door, unobtrusively watching the camp. Evin and I, meanwhile, rummaged through the backpack. It was mostly full of clothes, a few nuts and dried fruits, and – a mobile phone!

I almost cried for joy. 'Evin,' I whispered in excitement. 'A phone!'

'Let's see whether it's got a SIM card first,' she said, checking my enthusiasm.

My hands shaking, I opened up the phone. It *did* have a SIM card.

'Calm down,' Evin said. 'We're only going to take the card.'

'What?'

'Yes, just the card,' she repeated firmly. 'Don't be stupid, Farida. The SIM card is the most important thing. He'd notice if we took his phone.'

'Yes, but –'

'No buts.' She pocketed the card and put the phone back together.

'But we need a phone if we're going to do anything with the card!'

'We'll have to get one from somewhere else.'

Evin stuffed the clothes into the backpack. However hard it was to swallow, I realised that her strategy was right. A working SIM card was the most important thing. We'd find a phone sooner or later in the camp. If we wanted to succeed we mustn't rush. We had to act smartly and with consideration.

'OK,' I said. We left untouched the rest of the things in the backpack, including the nuts that I really fancied.

The other girls, too, found it hard to temper their impatience when we told them the good news. 'Why didn't you take the phone?' asked Besma, who was still badly wounded and close to tears again. 'We could have rung our parents!'

I shook my head. 'Evin's right. It would have been too dangerous. They'd have searched our container for the missing phone, and we'd soon be without both SIM and phone again.'

Besma pursed her lips, unwilling to accept fully the explanation. 'My mum will be very worried about me,' she said.

'I know. All our mums are worried. And we'll get in contact with them as soon as we get our hands on a phone.'

Evin and I already had an idea where we might find the phone we so badly needed. There was a room where the ISIS soldiers stored items seized from the enemy: clothes, munitions, boots, backpacks and – with a little luck – the dead men's mobile phones too. It was a sort of warehouse where the soldiers could help themselves. And in fact we were due to clean it soon.

Our hearts pounding, we entered the warehouse with our cleaning cloths for our next job. This time I was alone with Evin. Glancing hastily around the room, we immediately caught sight of three phones on a shelf. Would the soldiers notice if one was missing?

'We've got to risk it now,' I told Evin.

She nodded, and in a flash one of the mobiles had vanished beneath her cloak. We cleaned the room in record time and hurried back to the container.

Triumphantly we presented our booty to the other girls. They covered their mouths to stop themselves screaming in delight. 'You two are the best! Three cheers for you both! God bless you!' they whispered excitedly.

But Evin put a finger to her lips as a warning. 'Don't get overexcited now,' she said, 'or you'll immediately give us away.'

We waited until evening when it was quieter in the camp. Of course we could never be certain that one of our 'owners' wasn't standing by the door, ready to call for his girl, but at least the probability of this fell with every passing hour. To be absolutely sure that no one outside could hear us, Evin and I crept beneath a linen cloth with the mobile. Then we dialled the numbers we knew by heart. I had a whole string of them in my head: our home number, my father's and eldest brother's mobiles, as well as those of some relatives. But we soon had to admit that it was pointless. All the lines were dead.

'Well,' I said, disillusioned, 'I suppose it's only logical. I mean, they collected up all the mobiles.' What had I been expecting? That the village was free again now and ISIS had returned all the phones? Secretly, I'd of course nurtured the hope that one or other of them had managed to take their SIM card into captivity, or wherever they were.

'We haven't got anyone any more,' Besma cried. 'They're all dead.'

'No, they're not dead,' I countered. 'They just don't have their phones on them. We don't have our phones any more, either, do we?'

The others said nothing. It was a difficult moment for us all, as we suspected that the catastrophe which had befallen our community was greater than we'd previously assumed. Where were our families? Was there really nobody left we could ask for help?

'Maybe we have to bribe the boys who I heard saying they were in contact with people smugglers,' I thought out loud.

The other girls looked at me in horror. 'What do you plan to bribe them with? We don't have anything.'

I saw that it was an absurd plan. We really did have nothing to offer them. Nothing apart from ourselves. Did one of us have to offer herself up to prise from them the information we needed? I'm still ashamed today that such thoughts occurred to me. But desperation sometimes causes people to come up with ideas that are normally unthinkable.

'I've got an uncle who lives in Germany,' Evin said, interrupting my thoughts.

'Of course,' I recalled. 'Your uncle Khalil, isn't it?' I'd met her uncle and his family when they visited out village. He came regularly once a year and had also accompanied us on our pilgrimage to Lalish.

'Do you know his number?'

Evin screwed up her eyes and thought hard. But she had difficulty recalling it from her memory. 'All I remember is that it begins 0049,' she said.

'Think,' I urged her. 'You've *got* to remember it.'

'Yes, wait . . . The number used to be on the pinboard beside the phone . . .'

'You mean the one in red ink?' I closed my eyes and tried to remember too. I'd been to Evin's house often enough and, as I've said, I have a particular relationship to numbers. I can recall them far more easily than names. All of a sudden I saw the sequence of digits in my mind. 'I think I've got it!' I said.

By joining forces we reconstructed the number we thought was correct. Evin punched it into the mobile. Would the credit on the phone be sufficient for an international call? A person answered but we didn't understand what they were saying. It wasn't Evin's uncle. Disappointed she hung up. 'It's the wrong number,' she said.

I thought about this. Where could the error be? I saw the number in my head again. Had I got a digit muddled? 'Replace the seven with a one,' I told Evin.

She dialled the new number and suddenly we heard a familiar voice. 'Is that Khalil Aziz? Uncle Khalil?' Evin asked.

'Who's that?'

'It's Evin.'

'Evin! We've been so worried about you! Where are you?'

'Uncle, we don't have much battery or credit left. So I'm going to be brief. Me and seven other girls were abducted and are being held captive in an ISIS military camp. The camp's about an hour out of Deir ez-Zor, near the Omar oilfield.'

'Heavens! Leave this with me,' he said. 'I'll try to find someone who can get you out of there. I'll call you with news when I have some,' he promised.

'Did you hear that? He's going to send for help,' Evin said when she hung up, and we all embraced each other. We were almost bursting with confidence and rekindled hope. Finally we'd established contact with the outside world. Finally someone from one of our families knew where we were. Finally someone was looking after us. Now we were convinced that everything would turn out fine.

The anticipation that Evin's uncle was organising our rescue from Germany gave us all a boost. The day after our phone call was one of the few in the camp when my friends and I had a smile on our faces. It wouldn't have taken much for us to start singing as we went about our cleaning jobs.

Since our last encounter I'd heard nothing from Azzad. He was probably still nursing the wound on his midriff which I'd hit so fiercely. Hopefully it would keep him in check until Evin's uncle had arranged everything. If he hurried, perhaps I'd never have to see Azzad again. I pictured him coming to our container to exact revenge on me, and me having already fled. Oh, how I'd love to see his face at that moment!

The following evening we sat around the mobile, waiting for Evin's uncle to call. I hope the battery doesn't die beforehand, I thought.

He rang an hour later. I beamed when I saw the German number; assured of success, Evin pressed the green button. 'Uncle Khalil?' she whispered conspiratorially. All of us were crowded round so as not to miss a single word of this crucial phone call.

'How are you?' Khalil Aziz asked.

'Fine, and you? Any news?'

'Yes, I've spoken to the man who would be the one to fetch you.' From the tone of his voice I could already tell that the news wasn't good. Evin and the other girls didn't seem to have noticed. Their faces glowed in anticipation.

'And?' my friend asked.

'The man says the place you're in is too dangerous.'

Their faces darkened. 'What does that mean?'

'It means he can't go there.'

The girls silently put their heads in their hands. We'd all heard what he'd said. And we couldn't believe it.

'But we need help,' Evin begged. 'Please . . .'

'Where you are, I'm afraid there's nothing I can do for you. I'm really sorry.'

Evin didn't say anything. She was crying softly.

'I know you're disappointed. But believe me, I've been ringing round all day long, trying everything,' her uncle insisted. 'You've got to escape from the camp. The man says that if you can get to somewhere else, a safer area, he can have you picked up.'

'But how's that going to work?'

'I don't know. Is there absolutely no possibility of escape?'

'No. Our container is right in the middle of the camp.'

Evin's uncle clearly didn't know what else to say. 'Try,' he encouraged us. 'I know you can do it. I'll give you the number of the man to contact when you're out. OK?'

He read out the number and Evin repeated it obediently. Just to be on the safe side I committed it to memory too.

'Do you promise me you'll try?'

'Yes,' she said sadly. 'Thank you, Uncle Khalil.'

'I'm really very sorry. I'd love to be able to do more for you,' he said. 'But it's not in my power.'

When Evin had finished her conversation, an awkward silence filled the container. All of us were bitterly disappointed. After banking so firmly on our rescue, we found it very hard to deal with the idea that nobody was going to come to our assistance in a hurry. Some of the girls started to weep silently to themselves. We felt abandoned by the outside world.

'At least we've got the phone number,' I reminded my friends so that they wouldn't lose hope altogether.

'Yes, but what good is it?' Sumeya asked. 'You know just as well as I do that it's impossible to get out of here.'

I mulled this over. Was it really impossible? Wasn't there any chance of escape? It would be extremely difficult at best. The front door of the container and the windows were always carefully locked by the soldiers. But still the main problem was that our container was in the middle of the camp, and thus surrounded on all sides by the soldiers' billets as well as guards. Even if we managed to find a way out of the container I didn't know how we'd be able to get beyond the security ring.

'All the same we have to try,' I said. 'You heard what Evin's uncle said. Our only chance is to break out and then call this man.'

'But it's much too dangerous,' Sumeya objected. 'If we do that they'll bring our mothers here from Tal Afar.'

'What?'

Sumeya bowed her head.

'That's what they threatened,' said Reva, who'd made the same mistake as Sumeya by giving away the names of her relatives. Now the ISIS soldiers were using this information to intimidate her. They threatened to fetch both girls' mothers here as 'replacements' if they dared attempt to flee. 'It's too dangerous,' Reva said as well. 'I could never forgive myself for bringing such misery on my mum.'

'But we don't even know if your mothers are still in captivity,' Evin protested. 'They could be lying to us.'

'You mustn't believe them,' I urged Reva and Sumeya. 'They're just trying to make us lose heart.'

The two girls were not convinced. 'But what if they do get our mothers?' Sumeya said. 'We can't take the risk.'

'Yes, we have to take the risk!' I challenged them. We couldn't agree. It was obvious to me that ultimately each of us would have to decide for herself what risks she was prepared to take. I, at any rate, was not going to be intimidated by any threats.

I racked my brains to try and identify a way of escaping, despite our strategically unfavourable situation. I examined the container from top to bottom, concentrating in particular on the windows and doors. We never normally used the door in the back room, and yet when I inspected it I got a big surprise: the bolt was merely tied up with wire, but not secured in any other way. My heart started to pound with excitement. How come we'd never noticed this before?

I unwound the wire and found that the bolt could easily be pushed to the side. I pushed the handle carefully and opened the door a crack, then shut it again quickly before anybody outside noticed. This couldn't be true!

'Hey, come here,' I called out to my friends, and showed them my discovery. They could barely believe what they saw either.

'Has that door basically been unlocked the whole time?' Evin asked, astounded.

'Yes,' I said. 'We just forgot it. Can you see now how fear makes you blind?'

They nodded.

'But if we rid ourselves of our fear, we can do it,' I tried to persuade them. From that moment on I became something like the group's escape officer, and all the girls called me 'Barack Obama'.

The very next day, 13 December 2014, chance came to our aid. The soldiers in our camp were engaged in heavy fighting with other jihadis. They came under such pressure that the chiefs even considered evacuating. To prepare for the move, the order for which could come at any time, the men brought us some abayas, the black full-length cloaks, with matching face veils that only left a slit for the eyes.

'This is a gift from heaven,' I whispered to Evin. 'These robes will make us invisible.'

All the men were ordered to the battlefront, Azzad included. Through the window I watched the camp slowly emptying. Only a few guards remained behind. 'Good riddance, Azzad!' I whispered, feeling happy. Everything was coming together: the unlocked back door, the abayas we needed as a disguise, the empty camp, the phone number of the man we could contact the moment we escaped. I realised that this was our historic chance.

As soon as peace had descended on the camp I rounded up my friends for a briefing. 'Either we take our chances now to escape, or never,' I told them. 'This is a unique opportunity. We'll never have another one like it again.'

'You're mad,' Sumeya countered. 'Don't forget they've left guards behind.' One of the guards was Sumeya's 'owner', another Reva's. They'd definitely be requesting their girls this evening. ISIS men who owned women always took advantage whenever they had a moment of peace. So I thought I knew what they were trying to say.

'We'll wait till you're back, of course,' I said. 'We won't leave you alone.' But I'd misunderstood them.

'I'm not coming with you,' Sumeya said, looking shamefully at the floor. 'Please understand me – it's just too dangerous.'

I looked at her aghast. 'You're not serious?'

'I've told you – if they did anything to my mum I'd never be able to forgive myself.'

'Sumeya's right. I'm not coming either,' Reva announced.

I nodded slowly. Although I found it hard to comprehend their decision, it was based on solid reasoning. If they elected not to escape then I had to accept that. 'Is there anyone else who thinks it's too risky?' I asked the others.

The girls remained silent.

'So the rest of you are in, then? Quite sure?'

'Yes,' they murmured, nodding.

'Good,' I said. 'We'll try tonight.'

We waited impatiently for evening to come. Reva and Sumeya were indeed summoned by their 'owners' shortly after dusk, the men making use of the peaceful time in the camp to enjoy their girls. For us it could only be an advantage if these two guards were distracted. All the same I had a bad conscience when my two friends put on their headscarves to leave. 'Are you quite sure that we shouldn't wait for you?' I asked again, before they left the container.

They nodded. 'It's a reckless plan. I'd advise you to abandon it too. They've set up guards around the camp. And if they see you they'll shoot,' Sumeya warned.

'Maybe,' I said. 'But it's a risk we have to accept, or we'll remain slaves forever.'

'I'd rather be shot,' little Besma piped up.

'Best of luck,' Reva whispered, giving me a hug. Sumeya embraced me and the other girls too, before going out.

'Same to you,' I said.

After the two had left, I explained to the girls the escape plan I'd worked out in my head. 'We have to split up into groups of two,' I said. I'd thought it all through very carefully.

'Why?'

'It increases our chances of getting away. If the guards see two of us, they'll chase after them. Then the others can run away.'

'So it increases the chances, but only for four of us,' Sila said.

'That's right.'

She sighed. 'That's not great, is it?'

'It's much shrewder than all six of us going the same way and all being caught together,' I replied. 'At least four will escape.'

The girls nodded comprehendingly. 'OK, we'll do it that way. Which route will we take then, Mr Obama?'

I'd given that due consideration too. From our cleaning tasks we all knew the camp pretty well, so I was able to give my friends detailed instructions. 'We'll all head north-east,' I said, as I suspected that this would be the quickest way of leaving ISIS-held territory. 'But we'll take different routes. Nase and Pervan will go to the right of the assembly hall, Sila and Besma to the left, while Evin and I will chart a middle route, so that we're as far away from each other as possible if they do nab two of us. But all of us have to give the hall itself a wide berth, because there's almost always someone sitting on guard there. As soon as we've left the camp we must try to find each other again.'

'OK,' Evin said calmly. But from the way she was frowning I could tell that she was very concerned about whether the plan would work. 'When do we get going?'

I hesitated. I'd originally thought that around midnight would be best. But now that at least two of the men were distracted with our friends, a more opportune moment had perhaps presented itself. It had also just started to rain; the loud drops were hammering on our roof. The noise would afford us additional cover. So there was no time to lose. 'It would be best if we left now,' I said. 'While it's still raining . . . and . . .'

'Yes,' Evin said, before I could say my thoughts out loud. 'Reva and Sumeya have given us a gift, so let's make the most of this valuable time.'

We put on our abayas and tied the face veils behind our heads so that we looked like black ghosts. At night you were virtually invisible in these robes, which was perfect for us. We didn't wear anything on our feet because we only had slippers, which were fine for cleaning inside, but totally unsuitable for running. They'd also make a noise with each step we took. To be on the safe side, therefore, we carried them. Under my cloak I'd tied our greatest treasure, the mobile phone, tightly to my body. But the others had also learned the crucial number by heart. In case we lost each other in our flight, somehow they still might be able to call our contact for help – at least that was what we reckoned.

I unwound the wire from the handle again, pushed the bolt to the side and tentatively pressed down on the handle. A cool, rainy waft of air greeted me from outside; it had turned quite chilly. I opened the door a little further and peered outside. As I'd suspected, the lights were still on in the assembly hall, which was visible from here. Glancing behind me, I saw the wide, anxious eyes of my friends, peeping out from their black veils. Each girl was holding the hand of her escape partner.

'Are you all ready?' I whispered.

'Yes,' they replied. Evin and I stepped outside first. We were enveloped by cold, damp and darkness. And yet I felt a huge sense of euphoria. I really thought it would work this time. This escape attempt had been far better planned than anything we'd ventured before. It simply had to succeed.

We hurried through the camp. Soon Evin and I had lost sight of the other girls. To ensure we stayed together we kept a hold of each other's hand as we dashed past the containers in which we'd been the victims of so much violence. Now they stood there dark and deserted, and yet they still terrified us, for any moment a soldier could step out from behind and stop us, crushing our dream.

We recoiled in fear when Evin unexpectedly knocked over a metal bucket in the darkness. It rolled along the ground with a loud clunk. Evin stopped and listened. Had anyone heard? 'Come on,' I whispered, pulling her away. 'Don't stop now – we've got to get out of here as fast as possible.'

We crouched as we crept past the assembly hall, keeping our distance, and we finally reached the perimeter of the container settlement undetected – a partial victory at least. Beyond lay an expanse in total darkness: the desert. We waited here for the other girls to arrive; this had been our arrangement. And the other four made it too. We all held hands so nobody got lost in the darkness, with Evin and me going at either end. Then we started to run. We ran blindly in our bare feet, unable to see where we were heading. I didn't feel the wet and cold on my soles.

Suddenly I could hear dogs barking somewhere nearby. The ISIS soldiers must have positioned the animals outside the camp as an alarm against intruders. Were they on leashes? Or were they roaming around freely? Would they snap at us and tear us to pieces with their teeth? I couldn't see the dogs anywhere, but they were making a hell of a row with their barking. Oh no, I thought. They would wake all the guards in the camp, who would immediately know something was wrong and would start hunting for us. We ran as quickly as we possibly could.

There was no light anywhere ahead of us. But we could hear the dogs coming closer. They must be roaming freely. Little Besma stumbled, but I grabbed her arm and yanked her roughly along with me. If we fell behind now we were finished.

We ran through the rain until we couldn't run any longer. I don't know how long we kept it up, but it felt like an eternity. All of us were undernourished and in bad health, and eventually we were forced to slow our tempo. We were completely out of breath, coughing and panting, but we couldn't hear the dogs any more, thank goodness. The camp was some way behind us. When I looked around I could still make out the light of the assembly hall in the distance.

We seemed to have nobody on our tail. I hardly dared believe it. Had we really managed to lose the men and the dogs? But now wasn't the time to ponder this. 'Come on, we've got to continue,' I urged the girls.

We trudged through the darkness. The rain grew increasingly heavy. To avoid going in a circle by mistake, we persistently headed in one direction, without knowing where it would take us.

In the end we came to an asphalt road and decided to follow it. But we walked alongside the road rather than on it, so that if a vehicle came past the driver wouldn't be able to spot us immediately. Fortunately there wasn't much traffic that night. But whenever we heard the drone of an engine, we'd crouch in the scree by the roadside. Our black robes helped us blend into the night-time landscape.

At some point we came across a sign saying 'Hasakah'. Now at least we knew we were heading towards the Kurdish city. We used the road to guide us, continuing to tramp beside it in the rain. Soaked to the bone and frozen, we kept going unstintingly, all through the night.

When dawn came I sent a quick prayer heavenwards. 'Lord, You have allowed us to escape. I thank You,' I whispered as I turned to the sun. 'Please continue to help us. Do not abandon Adam's children any more.'

Now we started to see the odd house by the roadside, which was risky for us. We needed a hiding place before anyone saw us. As day had broken we couldn't continue walking.

We found the shell of a building, standing close to another house that was obviously lived in. As soon as we'd crept inside this shell we realised how exhausted we were from our night-time march. Water dripped from our clothes, but we had nothing to change into. Shivering with cold and our teeth chattering, we hugged each other to share a little warmth. We were in urgent need of refreshment after our exertions, but unfortunately had nothing to eat or drink.

While the other girls rested, I took out our mobile phone. Now was the time to call the number Evin's uncle had given us. The battery was low and there was hardly any credit left. The phone wouldn't work for much longer. Hopefully we'd got far enough away from the military camp for the man to come and fetch us.

Evin watched me dial the number with trembling fingers. It was an uplifting moment as we really believed we'd made it.

A man called Mustafa Hamu answered. I introduced myself and mentioned Evin's Uncle Khalil, who he'd spoken to already.

The man didn't sound surprised. He was neither friendly nor unfriendly, but very businesslike. 'When did you escape?' he asked.

'Last night.'

'Where are you now exactly?'

'I can't say for sure. In the shell of a building on the road to Hasakah,' I explained.

'Don't you know the name of the settlement?'

'It's not a settlement, just a few houses dotted around.'

'That's too vague. I need a concrete address to find you. You've got to ask in one of the houses there, or keep going to Hasakah.'

My heart sank. 'But we're absolutely exhausted,' I said. 'We don't have any dry clothes or anything to drink.'

'I'm afraid I can't help you otherwise. You have to understand, I can't get drawn into an adventure like that. So come up with an idea and call me back.'

'Please, we can't. We've barely any credit left on the phone.'

I couldn't understand why the man was so uncooperative. My friends and I had risked our lives to escape from the camp. He couldn't just leave us in the lurch like that. But he refused to change his mind. 'You're in the middle of ISIS territory,' he reminded me before hanging up.

Evin and I looked at each other in despair. We realised that this man was not at all interested in our plight. He was a businessman, coolly calculating his entrepreneurial risk. After this conversation the two of us felt pretty disillusioned.

'It's hopeless. As soon as it gets dark we've got to keep going,' I said.

Evin shook her head, pointing at little Besma, whose whole body was shaking. 'I'm cold,' the young girl complained. But her head felt burning hot when I touched it with my hand.

'She's got a temperature,' I said.

'Yes, she desperately needs something to drink. Dehydrated and overheated, there's no way she'll be able to walk any further tonight.'

'What are we going to do, then?' There was no question of abandoning our friend; either we made it together or we didn't make it at all.

'We've got to try and get help,' Evin said.

'Where?'

'Maybe from that house.'

I didn't much like the idea. 'Who knows what sort of people live there,' I protested.

'But we don't have any other choice! Besma's too weak to walk. And we can't carry her the whole way either – we don't have the strength.'

'OK,' I agreed, biting my lip. 'We'll ask at the house. But not right away. Let's take a good look first before we do anything.' I was determined to avoid falling blindly into a trap. If a bunch of ISIS people lived there we'd recognise them by their vehicles, weapons and clothes. Then we'd have to seek help elsewhere.

'That's what we'll do,' Evin said. 'I reckon we'll have the best view of the property from the roof.'

We climbed upstairs together and hid behind one of the windows. At first glance the building looked like a perfectly normal house; we couldn't see anything unusual. Voices and cries kept drifting over to us. But we couldn't see any of the occupants.

After a while a white Kia entered the drive and a man stepped out. He was fairly tubby, with short hair and a short beard, and was wearing civilian clothing. He didn't look like a soldier. Perhaps he was the father of a family living in the house. And then a woman appeared at the door with two children. She wasn't veiled ISIS-style either, but just wearing a dress and headscarf. We breathed a sigh of relief.

'It's a family,' Evin said. 'Perfectly normal people.'

'True, but don't forget they're living in the middle of ISIS-held territory,' I pointed out. 'They must have come to some sort of arrangement with them, otherwise they wouldn't be able to stay here. After all, we weren't able to stay when the ISIS men came, were we?'

'You could be right,' she said pensively. 'But maybe as far as ISIS is concerned they're of the right faith and that's why they're being left in peace.'

'We don't know what these people will think about Yazidis. They might regard us as devil worshippers.' As I listened to myself speak

I realised how mistrustful I'd become of all Muslims and the world in general. I could hardly believe that there were decent people among them too.

'Let's watch the house a little longer,' I begged Evin. Having got this far I really didn't wish to take any more risks.

'All right, but remember that Besma and the rest of us urgently need water.'

We spent all day on the lookout. I noted that a total of seven people lived in the house: the father, mother and their five children – three boys and two girls. One of the sons was still very small, the others were of school age. One of the daughters was roughly my age, so almost an adult. None of them wore clothes that were militantly Islamic, which I found somewhat reassuring. Over the course of the day I watched them go about their routines: cooking, eating, doing the washing, driving off in the car and coming back, doing homework. I envied them; how wonderful it must be to be able to lead a totally normal life.

When the sun set I was still unsure whether we ought to reveal ourselves. It was and remained a risk I really didn't want to take. Perhaps we might make it to Hasakah on foot after all. But Besma's condition had by now grown even worse. She was glowing like a stove and talking nonsense in her feverish delirium. The other girls were very feeble too, and shivering with cold. So Evin urged me to try it. She glanced at our little friend. 'If we don't get her water and dry clothes immediately she's not going to make it. We're sinning against her!'

'OK. Let's give it a go,' I agreed, gritting my teeth.

At first we considered sending a delegation to ask for help, but then agreed that we were all going to risk it together. The moon had just risen above the horizon, so we said a short prayer before leaving our hiding place. Standing in a row, we turned to face the heavenly body and whispered the formulas that our fathers and grandfathers had taught us. 'Lord, have mercy upon us,' I begged Melek Taus and the group of angels who decided on our destiny at the autumn gathering. 'Take pity on us. We have suffered enough.'

'Amen,' the girls muttered. 'May God protect the faith. God is our witness: we have never betrayed our faith.'

Then we tied our face veils behind our heads and adjusted our abayas. Once more covered from head to toe in our still damp, black robes, we stepped out into the road. Evin and Sila supported Besma, as she couldn't walk unassisted. It wasn't just me who felt uneasy as we slowly approached the house that stood there dark and silent in the dusk. The only light came from behind the drawn curtains in the windows. Evin looked at me and I nodded. Pluckily, she knocked at the door.

I couldn't help trembling when I heard footsteps in the hallway: men's footsteps. The man of the house opened the door to us. Behind him stood his eldest son, a teenager. They stared at us as if we'd come down from the moon; we must have looked like extraterrestrials. All six of us fell to our knees at the same time, even Besma in her fever.

'Sir,' I addressed the man, 'we're in desperate circumstances and we need your help. Our lives are in your hands.'

'Who are you?' he asked, perplexed.

I'd already thought that it would be pointless to lie to him. It was too obvious who we were and where we'd come from. We had to tell him the truth. 'We were held captive and ran away,' I said.

I saw fear in the man's face, which wasn't surprising as the situation was dangerous for him too. 'What's it got to do with me?' he asked gruffly. He wanted to be rid of us as soon as he could.

'We urgently need your help,' I repeated. 'Water, food . . .'

'That's impossible!' he said. 'I ought to go right now and inform the military leadership that you're here.'

Evin looked him in the eye. 'If you're a good man and believe in a god, then help us,' she implored him. 'If not, hand us over to ISIS.'

The man mulled this over; he was clearly struggling with our request. 'Things aren't that simple. The ISIS soldiers are always passing by this way, demanding food and drink,' he said. 'What if they saw you?' Father and son exchanged uncertain glances.

'Maybe we'll get a reward from their families if we help them,' the son whispered. This argument seemed to be conclusive.

'All right, maybe you can come in for a bit,' said the father, who now introduced himself as Abu Yousef. 'Then we'll have a think about it.'

'Thank you,' I said, but hesitated before stepping over his threshold. The man had a financial interest in us. Could we really trust him? It surely wasn't advisable to wait any longer outside his door where the whole world could see us, but by entering his house we were delivering ourselves into his hands. If his intentions were malicious he could imprison us again, hand us over or sell us on. We went in nevertheless.

In the hallway my nostrils were tickled by the aroma of freshly cooked rice. What a wonderful, familiar smell, the smell of home. 'What's going on?' Abu Yousef's wife called from the kitchen and put her head round the door. She was more than surprised to see six girls veiled in black in her hallway. After her husband had given her the lowdown on us she looked concerned.

'You poor girls,' she said impulsively when we removed our veils and she saw our young faces. 'You're half frozen – your lips have turned blue. No wonder, given the weather out there . . .' She stopped and turned to her husband. 'Isn't it far too dangerous to put them up here?'

'Yes, we have to be careful,' he acknowledged. 'The best thing would be to take them into the back room and pull down the blinds so no one can see them from outside.' His wife nodded and showed us the way.

'We've got the phone number of a man who can pick us up,' I said.

'That's good.' Abu Yousef asked me to give him the number I knew by heart. I dictated it to him, as well as that of Evin's uncle in Germany.

Then I followed the others into one of the children's rooms, where the wife had already pulled down the roller blinds. For a split second

I was assailed by the recollection of the room in the Syrian slave dealer Abu Dua's house, where the roller blinds had been down permanently. But I tried to get a grip and not to panic. It's different here, I told myself. The blinds had been closed for our protection.

Once the woman of the house had got over her initial shock, she slipped into the role of hostess. She brought us bandages and a bowl for us to wash our bloody feet after the long march. She put our abayas in the washing machine and brought us new clothes that belonged to herself and her eldest daughter. 'My goodness, you're brave girls,' she acknowledged. 'You did very well to run away from there!'

I smiled with pride and embarrassment. It was the first time I'd been praised rather than beaten for my rebellious behaviour.

'Now you just rest here with us.'

'That's very kind of you,' I said as I helped her put cold compresses on Besma to bring down her temperature. Evin gave the girl water and Sila washed her damaged feet. She was in a very bad state and shivering continually. We swaddled her in thick woollen blankets.

'I bet you're starving,' our hostess said. 'I'll make you something to eat.'

'That's not necessary,' I said politely, although even the thought of food made my stomach rumble.

'Yes it is,' she insisted. 'You are our guests.'

Now I was certain that fortune was on our side. We'd found shelter with decent people. I wanted to cry out of sheer relief. 'Thank you, dear woman,' I said, kissing her hand.

Soon afterwards we were washed, in clean clothes and having dinner around a large tablecloth on the floor. I finally felt human again – and felt, too, that I was being treated like one. Our hostess had employed all her culinary skills for us. We were given rice with chicken, salad, houmous and falafels, as well as Sprite and Coca-Cola. Our mouths were watering at the sight and smell of all these delicacies we'd been without for so long. All the family members were now behaving as if we were state guests.

'I've spoken to your uncle Khalil and Mustafa Hamu,' Abu Yousef said. 'They will do all they can to organise your rescue.'

'Thank you,' I said with tears in my eyes. 'We'll never forget you for this. You are a good man, Abu Yousef.'

But he made a dismissive gesture, as if his hospitality were a matter of course – even though he'd wanted to send us away at first. I puzzled over what could have changed his mind. Was he doing as his son suggested, and asking for money?

'Here you are safe, at any rate,' he said grandiosely. 'If needs be I will defend you against ISIS with my own hands. Now you are free people once more.'

We thanked him many times as we ate everything we could get our hands on. Although we were ashamed at helping ourselves in such a way, I have to admit that no meal had ever tasted as good as this one: our first dinner in freedom.

We stayed at the house for a few days, spending most of our time in the back room. I was used to sharing a small room with my friends, of course, but this time it felt very different, for we were free people. Our door wasn't locked!

Abu Yousef's children would come to see us occasionally. They were extremely excited by our sudden appearance in their house and wanted us to tell them the story of our escape over and over again, drilling us with questions. 'But weren't you afraid of going away on your own at night? What would you have done if you hadn't found our house?'

I was very willing to tell them everything. They were wide-eyed, but ultimately they couldn't begin to imagine what we'd been through. My stories were like an action film for them. Sometimes they asked questions we couldn't answer so easily, for example: 'Where are your parents? Aren't they missing you?' Then we'd become very pensive and quiet. All of us were weighed down by worries about our parents and siblings. We'd heard in the meantime that our village was still occupied by ISIS, but we didn't know how our relatives were, or whether they were even still alive.

Although Besma's recovery was very slow, it was steady. We managed to lower her temperature with the cold compresses and soon her eyes were full of life again in her pretty, pale face. Indeed, they looked almost happy when she realised that we were over the worst. 'Have we really done it, Farida?' she asked me. 'Really? Are you sure that absolutely nothing can go wrong now?'

'Ninety-eight per cent sure,' I said. 'The rest is a breeze for brave girls like you and me. Mustafa Hamu is going to send a driver to pick us up from here.'

'What then?'

'Then we'll go to Hasakah, and from there back into Iraq.'

'Back to our families?'

'Yes, to our families.'

She sighed. 'It's going to be so lovely to see my mum again,' she said. 'Are you dreaming about that too?'

'Yes,' I admitted. To hug my mother again was my greatest desire. And of course my father, my brothers and my dear friend Nura. But where were they? A queasy feeling crept up on me when I recalled our last few moments together. Since then I'd had absolutely no news about my family. Were they still alive? The shots we'd heard from inside the school building echoed in my head, and an ice-cold shiver ran down my spine. No, I didn't want to think like that. I kept hoping that, just like me, my dear parents and brothers had found some way to escape the thugs.

But my fear for them grew. I was particularly concerned by the fact that neither Abu Yousef nor Evin's Uncle Khalil could establish any contact with them. From the scraps of conversation I picked up when our host was on the phone, I knew that both of them were trying as best they could to find our families. Abu Yousef, because he probably wanted a suitable reward for his hospitality, and Evin's uncle because he couldn't afford Abu Yousef's and Mustafa Hamu's services on his own.

Finally, on the third day, Abu Yousef came to our door in the morning and said we should get ready to leave. We immediately put on our own old clothes and black robes.

Around midday a pickup arrived at the house. Our host spoke with the driver that Mustafa Hamu had sent. We spent an age waiting in the back room.

But then everything happened very quickly. Abu Yousef came and said he'd sorted everything out. He accompanied us to the front door. The driver was already back in his cab and manoeuvred the vehicle a little closer to the front door. 'Have a safe journey,' our host said as we departed. 'I hope you're all reunited with your families!'

'Thank you, Abu Yousef. All the best for you and your family too,' we replied. Then we hurried over to the pickup and climbed onto the cargo bed, which was full of rolls of cloth, crates and plastic tarpaulins we could hide under.

I was bursting with excitement as we set off. Our destination, the Kurdish city of Hasakah, where Mustafa Hamu lived, was around two hundred kilometres to the north. Hopefully everything would be fine.

Each time the vehicle slowed down I held my breath. I prayed to Melek Taus that we wouldn't be stopped by a roadside check, especially not one where they inspected the cargo. If the self-appointed holy warriors found us there they'd take us captive again immediately. Which would put our ordeal back to square one.

For a long time our journey was quiet. As we were hidden by tarpaulins I couldn't see where we were going. But I think that the driver had chosen certain farm tracks to avoid the controls. I was slightly amazed that it was all going so smoothly, for in my imagination ISIS had installed checkpoints everywhere throughout the territory it controlled. But that was clearly not the case.

Then, however, the pickup suddenly came to a stop and I could hear the driver negotiating with a man. I didn't understand what the two of them were saying. Moments full of anxiety passed, in which we didn't know what would happen. When the vehicle started moving again I took hold of Evin's sweaty hand. We breathed a sigh of relief. Had the driver given the man money to stop any further bother?

That seemed the most likely explanation. Presumably the bribe he had to pay was included in our fare.

After about three or four hours' drive, which felt unbelievably long to me and the other girls, we reached the suburbs of Hasakah, a city on the edge of the Kurdish area, and not far from the Iraqi border. Like Sinjar, it had been overrun by jihadis in August and was still under ISIS control, although not all parts of the city. Mustafa Hamu's house was in an area that ISIS hadn't conquered.

I was most concerned about this last part of the drive, for I assumed that ISIS had installed blockades on the boundaries of the territory they had command over, to control the coming and going of all vehicles. Would the self-styled holy warriors let us pass? As I'd anticipated, we stopped at one of these checkpoints. Our driver got out and slammed the door shut. He greeted the guards checking him. He clearly knew them because he called them by name. My heart was in my mouth. Was he one of them? Would he hand us over or sell us? After a short while the man got back in and we were on our way again. Ten minutes later we stopped outside the house where Mustafa Hamu lived with his family. Our rescuer pulled back the plastic tarpaulin.

'Welcome, dear girls,' he greeted us. The Yazidi people smuggler had a moustache and wore the traditional white clothes with a jacket and an Arabic scarf on his head with a headband. 'My warmest congratulations! You made it!'

Mustafa Hamu entertained us royally. Or perhaps everything put in front of me just seemed fit for a king after such a long time in captivity. Once more I ate three times the usual amount. My friends didn't hold back either. We apologised, saying we had to replenish our stores. And in truth we were emaciated. 'Tuck in, girls!' his wife encouraged.

The couple put us up in a guest room where, by the looks of things, a number of visitors of our sort had taken shelter in the past, people who Mustafa Hamu had helped escape. I was sure the man earned a huge amount of money for his services. And yet I can't regard his work as anything but honourable. Without a professional helper like him we'd never have been able to get away from the 'Islamic State'.

We showered and tried to get some sleep. But none of us could manage a wink. We were far too excited, for that night we would be heading further towards our homeland. Mustafa Hamu was going to take us to Derik on the Iraqi border.

'But we don't have any passports,' I pointed out.

'It doesn't matter,' he said. 'The PKK, which controls the border on our side, and the Peshmerga on the Iraqi side have come to an agreement to let through Yazidi returnees even without passports.'

'How will they know we're Yazidis?' I asked, in all naivety.

'You can be sure they'll recognise you,' Mustafa Hamu said. He didn't explain any further what exactly he meant by that. But for the first time it dawned on me that everyone in this region knew how ISIS treated Yazidi girls, and what the men had done to us. I went bright red with shame, but in the same moment was angry that I felt this way. I mean, I hadn't done anything wrong. But would our families see it that way too?

Quite late that night Mustafa Hamu knocked at the door and informed us that it was time to leave. I couldn't fathom why we had to cross the border at night, when everything had supposedly been sorted out. Perhaps the 'agreement' he'd spoken about only worked with a few of Mustafa Hamu's personal acquaintances, who got paid for this.

We drove in his car for about half an hour before reaching the Euphrates. The bridge, which in peacetime led across the wide river, was blocked on the Syrian side. So we went further upstream to a slightly narrower point in the river, where a man in a small motorboat was waiting in the darkness. He must have been an acquaintance of Mustafa Hamu, for they greeted each other with a handshake. The man motioned to us to get into the boat. Mustafa Hamu made no move to come with us.

'Are we crossing the river illegally?' I asked him.

'No, it's all been sorted out,' he asserted.

'What do we do when we get to the other side?'

'People are expecting you.'

'Who?'

Mustafa Hamu shrouded himself in silence. Quite clearly he wanted to keep us in suspense which is why this vague announcement made us rather fidgety. Who would be welcoming us on the Iraqi side? Impatiently we got into the boat and the man started the motor.

Mustafa Hamu watched as we crossed the dark river. And I saw him wave goodbye to us from the bank. 'Best of luck!' he called out. 'I'll wait here until I'm certain that you've made it to the other side.'

We sailed across the broad expanse of water, accompanied by the rattling of the motor and its stench of diesel. An odd feeling of euphoria came over me at the thought of putting a foot in my homeland again. As we got closer to the other side I could make out a small group of people waiting for our arrival. My heart began thumping wildly. I felt for Evin's hand, which was just as cold as mine.

Somebody stretched out a hand, helping us out of the rickety boat and onto dry land. 'Farida,' said a familiar voice. And yet to begin with I didn't know who it was addressing me. 'Farida, is that you, my child?' he asked uncertainly. Then I recognised Uncle Adil, my father's elder brother. Although it was dark I could see that he'd lost a lot of weight and his face had become much more wrinkled than I remembered. I flew into his arms.

'Uncle Adil, Uncle Adil!' I cried, bursting into tears.

My uncle wept too. 'Thank the Lord that you're alive, child,' he said. 'We all thought you were dead.'

He held me very tight and stroked my head tenderly. 'You're alive, you're alive,' he mumbled again and again. 'Nothing else matters. Now everything's going to be all right again, Farida.'

But I barely heard what he was saying. I couldn't stop crying.

9

NO HOME, NOT ANYWHERE

All the girls were greeted by their relatives. Waiting for Evin were her brother Fansar and cousin Hamid, who'd come in the same taxi as my uncle. In the general excitement we barely had time to say a proper goodbye to the other girls. 'Thanks, Farida,' young Besma said to me before we went our different ways.

I gave her a conspiratorial nod. I knew that she wasn't referring to my part in helping her escape or the compresses, but to the episode with the scissors. 'Never forget how strong you are, my little friend,' I said, kissing her on the forehead.

Then I joined my uncle, Evin and the others in the taxi for the journey home. But we didn't go back home; home didn't exist any more. Uncle Adil informed me that I'd be staying with him and Auntie Hadia. They lived in a container in a refugee camp near the Kurdish city of Dohuk. Our village, Kocho, which was around 170 kilometres further south-west, was still occupied by 'Islamic State', he said. When I heard all of this I was gripped by worry. 'What about my parents?' I finally summoned the courage to ask.

'We don't know for sure, Farida. Your mother and the little boys are probably still imprisoned. We suspect they're in Tal Afar or Mosul.'

That was like a knife in my heart. My poor mother! Had she endured the same as me? Had she been sold as a slave too? I'd have been willing to offer myself immediately to the terrorists to take her place. For how could I enjoy my own freedom if she was still imprisoned?

'Don't despair, Farida,' my uncle said as if able to read my thoughts. 'We'll do all we can to liberate her from the clutches of ISIS.' He told me that now there were lots of men like Mustafa Hamu who had contacts in the Islamists' dominion and were offering their services for money. Hiring assistance for an escape cost several thousand dollars. 'But the Kurdish government is helping us to raise the money,' he said, trying to reassure me.

'What about Dad? And Delan and Serhad?' I asked anxiously.

'Serhad's in the camp with us.'

'Really?' That, at least, was good news. 'And Dad and Delan?'

'We haven't heard anything from them,' my uncle replied. 'We don't know if they survived or not.' He told me what I'd suspected and feared the whole time – that there had been mass shootings on the day when the Islamists attacked our village. 'But we don't know if they're among the victims,' he hurried to add. 'I mean, your little brother made it.'

My euphoria vanished in a flash. On hearing this unsettling news, the relief at having succeeded in our escape gave way to a black mood. It was like making a mockery of my own rescue; without my family, my new-found freedom was all of a sudden pointless. I couldn't bear to think about what might have happened and I buried the thought. Even before we reached the camp I understood that my old life was irrevocably over; it would never be the same as it once was.

We drove through the large gate at the bottom of the camp. Like the ISIS camp in Syria, it consisted of white living containers packed close together on a hillside, hundreds of them. Countless relatives and friends from Kocho were already waiting outside my uncle's container to greet us, the returnees. My fat aunt Hadia, who wasn't quite as fat as before, was there with her daughter, three-year-old

Rosa. The little girl ran up to me and both of them gave me a hug. 'Where have you been, Farida?' Rosa asked. 'Where are your parents and brothers?'

'I don't know . . . I haven't seen them in a long time,' I said, giving her a kiss.

'Are you going to stay with us now?'

'Yes, my sweet little girl. How I've missed you!'

'I'm so happy you're back,' my aunt said. 'The rest doesn't matter.'

I looked at her, then lowered my gaze in shame. I knew, of course, what she was referring to, but I didn't broach the subject. 'Yes,' I just said. 'I'm very happy too.'

'To begin with we thought that everyone who'd stayed in the village was dead. But then Serhad arrived, and now you. I'm sure the rest will turn up. You should have fled with us back then.'

'They will all return, hopefully, if the Lord so wishes.'

Then I saw my brother. Serhad wouldn't look me in the eye. He embraced me silently – and I knew that he'd suffered horrific experiences too. I longed to ask about my father, but I was so frightened of what I might hear. And in our culture, we avoid discussing matters which would cause pain to another.

'It's good you're alive, bro,' I said.

'It's good you're alive, sis,' he replied using the same words. 'I'm going to look after you from now on.'

I nodded. And I'll look after you, I thought, but didn't say it. I didn't want to deprive my brother of any more of the small residue of pride we both had. We would desperately need each other's support, but it wouldn't be easy to look each other in the eye.

I moved into the container that housed my uncle, aunt, their three small children and my sixteen-year-old brother, Serhad. It consisted of a single room we lived in during the day, and where at night we slept wrapped in woollen blankets on foam mattresses. In the entrance area there was also a cooking facility with two hotplates, as well as a bathroom with a loo and shower, which worked at least once a day.

Although our accommodation was very cramped and simple, I really didn't care. I was grateful to my aunt and uncle for taking me in and treating me and my brother like their own children. I made myself useful around the place whenever I could and helped my aunt clean the container. Or I'd lend a hand with the cooking. Our rations weren't exactly abundant, but there was always enough of the staples such as rice. So we tried to be creative and vary how we used them. In the clay oven that had been built at the edge of the camp, the women from Kocho baked our typical bread, which cooks on the oven wall until it's crispy. It smelled appetising and tasted delicious when I ate it again for the first time; it was like a little piece of our lost home.

My aunt was very good to me. As I learned, she, Uncle Adil and the children had only survived by a whisker. They'd stuck it out for days in the mountains without water or food until aerial bombing by the Americans created an escape corridor for them. 'There were times I thought we'd all die of thirst in the mountains,' my aunt said.

'Did you see Nura up there at all?' It was a question that had been on my mind the whole time. After all, my friend and her family had been among the first to leave Kocho for Sinjar. But I hadn't seen her in the camp yet.

'Nura? No,' Auntie Hadia said. 'But her family's here, or at least some of them.'

'Really?' What did that mean?

'As far as I know her mother and aunts are here.'

The following day I went looking for Nura's family. I soon found her mother, who'd taken shelter with relatives. She was in a container where the elderly women of Kocho were sitting together, drinking tea. I recognised many of them, at least vaguely. When Nura's mother realised who it was standing there she stared at me as if she'd seen a ghost. 'Farida?' she said uncertainly. 'Is it really you?'

'Of course it is!' I went over and gave her a kiss.

'My dear Farida,' she said, her eyes at once filling with tears. 'Have you heard anything of Nura?'

'What?' Why should I have? 'Isn't she here?'

Nura's mother told me that on the way to Sinjar their pickup had run into a checkpoint. 'They shot all the men,' she said. 'But the girls . . . all my daughters . . .' The woman couldn't say any more. She started to shake and had a crying fit. 'Those poor girls,' said one woman who'd put up her hair into a grey bun. She was wearing a white skirt, white blouse and a headscarf of the same colour. She looked straight through me, as if I weren't there. 'Our poor girls, defiled,' she lamented. 'They'll never be able to marry. No man will take them as their wife now. Their lives are ruined forever . . .'

I stormed out of the container like a scalded cat. Nura's mother hurried after me.

'Farida, wait!' she cried. 'Have you heard anything about Nura? Or her sisters? Did you see her where you were?'

'No,' I shouted, dashing to Auntie Hadia's container. My heart was pounding like mad and I could barely hold back the tears. I hid under my blanket, not wanting to see anyone. So that's what they really thought of us!

I fell sick. After about a week in the camp I felt feeble and miserable, and got a high temperature. I slept during the day, drawing the curtains inside the container and pulling the blanket over my head to allow me some peace from the world. With her rash comments it felt as if the old woman had severed the artery providing me with the will to live. Her savage judgement had broken my spirit, something that ISIS with all its cruelty hadn't managed.

Why should I show my face outside in the camp if people were gossiping about me behind my back? What point was there in going on living? I was a nothing, a nobody, a stranded girl, burdening my relatives. I had no future. Perhaps it would have been better not to return to this world.

My aunt thought my illness was a result of acute exhaustion after all our exertions. She tried to cheer me up and she never said a bad word about me, at least not in my presence. But I fancied I knew what she secretly thought of me. And that's why I felt so terrible.

My depression didn't escape Evin. 'Farida, what's wrong?' she demanded to know after I'd avoided her for a few days. 'What's troubling you?'

'Nothing,' I pretended. 'I'm just not feeling particularly well, that's all.'

'Farida, you can't go moping around the whole time,' my friend said. She told me that she too was smarting from the looks friends and relatives were giving her. It was inevitable that they were going to talk about us. Everyone in the camp knew what happened to abducted girls. 'Listen, we didn't fight all these battles with the jihadis only to allow ourselves to be browbeaten by our relatives,' Evin said. 'We mustn't stick our heads in the sand.'

'But we'll never be able to start a family. No one will want to have us.'

'That's what *they* say. But we've no idea what life has in store for us,' my friend corrected me.

The next time Evin visited me she came with someone I didn't know. The woman she brought to the container was around fifty years old, short, plump and brimming with energy. 'Are you Farida?' she asked me in Kurdish. And before I could answer she pulled me to her chest. 'I'm Afrah,' she said, 'Afrah Ibrahim. I'm the camp's social worker.'

I eyed her with suspicion. Afrah explained that she worked for a German organisation called Wadi, which supported women and girls in Kurdistan. In the past she'd fought against genital mutilation. She was clearly a Muslim, but she didn't wear any sort of veil, and tied up her medium-length dark hair with a slide. Afrah started to talk to Evin and me very openly about sexuality. She didn't mince her words and acted as if it were the most natural thing in the world. 'It's essential that you get checked up by a doctor,' she said, 'because your "owners" may have infected you with a disease.' We looked at her in horror.

'Don't worry,' Afrah reassured us. 'Every disease can be treated and cured. It's just important to spot them early enough.' She also implied that the same was true of a potential pregnancy.

I told her that throughout my time in captivity I hadn't had a regular period. 'That's due to the stress,' Afrah said. 'I'm sure everything's fine. But we ought to err on the side of caution. You owe it to your bodies to take good care of them.'

Evin and I soon realised that this woman was our ally. If the entire camp looked down at us, gossiping maliciously behind our backs about our supposed lost honour, then this woman understood us. She accompanied us to the doctor, listened to our concerns and treated us as equals when offering advice. It felt marvellous finally to be able to discuss our problems with someone, without it constantly being hinted at that our lives were ruined.

'So long as my mother remains in captivity, you are my mother,' I told her.

'And you're my daughter, Farida, my brave, spirited daughter.'

When I told Afrah about the gossip doing the rounds in the camp she flew off the handle. 'Don't listen to them,' she said. 'If you give licence to such thoughts it's like giving those ISIS criminals permission to abuse you again.'

I didn't know what she meant by that at first. But then I thought about it and it struck me how right she was in what she was trying to say: we mustn't give our tormentors the power to destroy our lives after the event too. In captivity we'd defied these criminals. But we had to resist them now as well. I understood that the fight was far from over. Every day we'd have to defend ourselves anew against this destructive force, which even from the past threatened to swallow us into a black hole.

Grasping this was a crucial step for me. No, I had refused to allow myself to be browbeaten in captivity. So I was not about to be browbeaten now by other people who thought I'd lost my 'honour'. 'Don't allow yourselves to believe it,' Afrah told us. 'You haven't lost your honour. On the contrary, you were brave and have every reason to go through life with your heads held high.'

My chest swelled with pride when she said things like that. Sometimes when I was strolling through the camp and heard people whispering, I would forget her words and feel utterly deflated. It was a constant battle. It *is* a constant battle. But I will win it, as I have all my battles up till now.

One evening someone hammered on our container with their fists. At the door stood a young boy holding a mobile phone. 'Does Farida live here?' he asked.

'Yes, that's me,' I said, getting up. We'd all been sitting around a gas stove, because the winter nights were very cold. The boy handed me the phone.

'Who is it?' I asked.

'Nura,' he said.

'Nura?'

'She wants to talk to you. Only you. She refuses to speak to my mother and aunts.'

I snatched the mobile from his hand and went off into a corner of the container. 'Nura, is it really you?' I asked excitedly.

'Farida!' I heard her dear, familiar voice.

'Where are you?'

'In Mosul. I've stolen a phone from my "owner".'

When I realised the meaning of her words I felt a cold shudder but hot at the same time. Nura was still a slave. She was calling me from her captivity. 'Nura!' I cried. 'My dear friend . . .'

'I miss you so much, Farida!' she said. 'Are you all right? I'm so happy you managed to escape. It's a great comfort to me to know that you're safe.'

'You've got to try too,' I implored.

'I have done, five times already. But they've always caught me again.'

'Then it'll work next time!' I encouraged her.

Nura told me she'd been sold in the marriage hall in Mosul. After Raqqa it was the largest marketplace for women and girls. The man who'd chosen her had made her his second wife. He'd treated Nura with great brutality when he forced her to have sex. His first wife hated her. Nura did the housework for both of them and they abused her continually, although the beatings she got from the lady of the house were the lesser evil.

I thought of my beautiful friend with her long brown hair and felt sick as she told me all of this. Nura was leading the life of a slave, like so many of us. 'You mustn't lose heart,' I told her. 'You've got to run away. Somehow you'll make it.'

'There's nothing I yearn for more than to be sitting with you up on the roof of your house and gazing down at your garden, Farida. That's my greatest desire.'

'We'll do it as soon as you're free,' I promised her. 'We'll go back to Kocho –'

'Someone's coming,' she interrupted me. 'I've got to go.' She hung up abruptly.

When I glanced up I saw that Nura's mother and two of her aunts had come into our container. They were looking at me in expectation. 'What did she say?' Nura's mother asked softly.

'She's fine,' I lied. 'She hopes to be with us soon.'

Nura's mother burst into tears. 'My poor girl,' she said. 'Did she say anything about her sisters?'

I shook my head.

Nura never called again. She must have been caught and they must have taken the phone off her. And yet I keep waiting for her.

Every day more returnees arrived at the camp. Women and children who'd managed to escape or ISIS had let free. Many of the girls of my age were on the verge of mental breakdown. I knew why. Now that they were free, quite a number of them tried to kill themselves out of shame. Or they started harming themselves.

Afrah had her hands full. She asked Evin and me to talk to the new arrivals and offer them comfort. 'The most important thing is to stop them blaming themselves for what's happened,' she said.

'We've got to help them put this horror behind them.' That was easier said than done, however. At night we'd often hear screams echoing around the camp when the girls had nightmares. It was as if our tormentors were grasping at us with their filthy hands even beyond captivity.

'Listen, we didn't do it intentionally,' I tried to convince my fellow sufferers. 'We are the victims, they are the criminals.' But I had the impression that my words didn't get through to many of them, who were so trapped in their self-incrimination. It was an arduous situation for us all, especially as neither Evin nor I were immune from this destructive self-reproach. We knew all too well how the other girls felt.

Some older women managed to escape too. One of them told me she'd met my mother in Kazel Tiu, a former Shia village near Tal Afar. The woman said that Yazidi boys were being trained as soldiers there. I immediately thought of my two little brothers and a horrific idea took root inside me: had ISIS succeeded in winning them over to their side? Were the teenagers now fighting for the thugs?

'They were after our children,' the woman said, confirming my worst fears. 'They brainwashed the boys; they were indoctrinated and had to pledge themselves to Islam. They left the girls in peace ideologically. But they were sexually abused, even the really young ones who were only nine or ten. They're criminals.' She spat in disgust. The last time she'd seen my mother was at the marketplace in Mosul. 'We were all held there. And then they decided who would remain imprisoned and who was allowed to go.'

I didn't know what to make of this information. Although I was happy finally to receive confirmation that Mum was still alive, what conditions was she living in? I told Serhad what I'd heard to give him a little hope too. He'd become withdrawn inside the camp and his behaviour was very aloof. All the time he wore such a grim expression that you scarcely dared approach him. But sometimes the mask slipped. 'Is that really true?' he said. 'I wish I could help her.'

'You can't,' I said gingerly. I didn't tell Serhad that our mother had been taken to the slave market. And I also kept quiet about the fact that ISIS were apparently giving our brothers military training. I didn't think he'd be able to cope with this information.

Even the details I did reveal well and truly rattled him. His first reflex was to join the Kurdish brigades in an attempt to liberate the area where my mother was. 'We need to reconquer Sinjar and Tal Afar,' he said. As part of a thrust in November the Kurdish units had advanced into the city of Sinjar, but were pushed back by the bitter resistance of the Islamists. 'Just imagine. If we'd kept hold of the city we'd now be able to march on to Kocho.'

'Serhad,' I pleaded, 'you're the only one I've got left. Please stay with me.'

'But we're talking about Mum!'

'Mum will be delighted when she comes back and finds you alive.' I reminded him that we couldn't assume we were going to see our father and Delan again. I'd never put it so directly before. But now I needed to be explicit to hold Serhad back. 'We need you, Serhad.'

Without saying a word he stormed out of the container, leaving me standing there.

It was a bleak, grey winter. If at first I'd thought our stay here in the refugee camp would be temporary, I slowly realised that our situation was not going to change in a hurry. Against all the prognoses to the contrary, the Sinjar region and Mosul were still under ISIS control. The front lines had hardened.

I grew more dissatisfied by the day with my existence in the camp. Ever since I'd arrived the prevailing mood had continually been one of Armageddon. If any camp inmate ever forgot for a second the horrors of the present, another would be quick to remind them. When so many traumatised people live in such close proximity, there's no spark of optimism. It was wearing me down.

But I was especially irritated by the fact that I had nothing to do here. I'd already missed half a year of school. After the summer holidays I should have been entering year 12 and sitting my leaver's exams in the months that followed. I'd even had the prospect of a grant. But now? Now my dream of becoming a maths teacher was over. Like everyone else here I was in limbo, suffering from a lack of prospects.

One day, I think it was the end of February or the beginning of March 2015, we were visited in the camp by a delegation from Germany, made up of representatives of the Yazidi community there as well as officials from one of the German states. Word soon got around that they were going to offer a limited number of people the opportunity to leave Iraq and travel to Germany. Apparently, young women and girls had a particularly good chance of being accepted onto the programme.

'Why don't you try, Farida?' my brother said.

'You want me to leave you here alone?'

'I'm not a child any more,' he said, peeved. 'I'll get by without you just fine.'

'And what about Mum?'

'When she's free we can come and join you. Life in Germany is supposed to be good.'

I thought about it. On the one hand, leaving my country behind seemed like a betrayal. On the other, I had to accept that I had absolutely no prospects here at the moment. I couldn't even finish my schooling. Instead I was getting wary looks from people. Maybe new opportunities would open up for me in Germany.

'You can try, at least,' my brother encouraged me. 'I'll try too.'

So we went to see the people responsible for registration. And Evin came as well. In the interview, which a German woman conducted with us through an interpreter, we told her the entire story of our abduction. 'You poor girls,' she said, shocked. 'I'm sure you'll be accepted onto the programme.'

After the delegation left, nothing happened for a few weeks. Spring came and the sun shone again with greater intensity onto the containers. But this had no effect on the atmosphere in the camp, which was just as bleak as in winter. We assumed that the foreigners who'd come to visit had forgotten us again, and we for our part gradually forgot them too.

But then, one day in April, Uncle Adil's mobile rang. On the other end of the line I could hear a man who spoke in a loud voice with a military tone. 'Yes, yes, that's right,' my uncle said, as I tried to read his face. 'She's my brother's wife . . . Yes, on this number . . . Let me know.'

When he'd hung up Serhad and I looked at him expectantly.

'Your mother's escaped,' he announced. Impulsively we shrieked with delight. 'She's under the Peshmerga's care.'

'When's she coming?' I asked.

'The soldiers are taking her to the hospital first. They'll let me know as soon as she's arrived.'

This was the best news I'd heard in my life. Mum was free. I felt as if someone had removed black veils from my eyes. I went out of the container, turned to the sun and whispered, 'Thank you! Thank you, my Lord. Thank you for having answered my prayer.'

For the rest of that day I was on cloud nine. I stayed close to my uncle so as not to miss the call that would tell us when Mum had arrived in Dohuk. I checked several times to make sure his mobile was charged and the volume set correctly. Everything was working perfectly. We were just waiting for the call. That night I also stayed close to the phone, which my uncle of course hadn't switched off. I couldn't sleep a wink.

'Perhaps you ought to call them back?' I suggested the following morning. But he didn't have any credit. The much-anticipated call finally came on the afternoon of the following day. A soldier informed us tersely that Mum had arrived at the hospital.

We took the bus into town; it took around an hour. As I looked out the window and watched the barren, flat landscape of southern Kurdistan pass by, my mind went into a spin. What condition would I find my mother in? Would I see my brothers too? Or had ISIS snatched them? I looked over at Serhad, who was sitting beside me, still wearing that same grim expression. He didn't say a word the entire journey.

At Dohuk hospital we were checked by Peshmerga soldiers. There was a ward specifically to treat those returning from ISIS captivity.

Glimpsing the people there gave me the creeps. Many of them were suffering from malnutrition and the consequences of terrible abuse. My uncle headed purposefully to a bed where a woman lay. It took me a moment to realise who it was.

'Mum!' I cried, horrified. My mother was nothing but skin and bones. She looked terribly old and emaciated. Her dark hair was streaked with grey and deep furrows lined her face, even though she was only forty. A tube stuck out of her arm.

'Farida, my child,' she said weakly. 'Serhad. How lovely to see the both of you again.'

Kneeling beside her bed, I took her bony hand in mine and kissed it. 'You don't know how much I've missed you, Mum. What's wrong with you?'

'Nothing,' she insisted. 'It's just that I haven't had anything to eat recently.' She attempted a feeble smile. 'I'll be fine again soon. The most important thing is that the two of you are all right, my dear children.' She wept. Then, from the far side of the room two adolescent boys approached. They were my brothers: twelve-year-old Keniwar and Shivan, who'd now turned fourteen. Both of them had grown quite a bit since I'd last seen them in the summer, when they were strong, energetic boys, full of mischief. Now they were skinny, and unable to look anybody in the eye. They were not the same naughty kids I once knew.

'Is that you, Farida?' Shivan asked in what was now a deep voice. He shyly let me embrace him. But it felt as if I'd become a stranger to them over all these months we hadn't seen each other. Keniwar, too, hugged me rather hesitantly. Happily they were less reticent about physical contact with Serhad.

'What happened to Dad and Delan?' they asked him. 'You were driven away with them, weren't you?'

Serhad shook his head sadly. 'I wasn't with them,' he said. 'The last time I saw Dad was in the playground. But then they put me into a different lorry . . .'

'Where did they take you?' Shivan probed.

Serhad swallowed. 'They drove us up to a field,' he said. 'We thought they were going to let us free at first. But we had to get out and line up alongside a pond . . .' His eyes glazed over.

'And then?' my mother asked.

'Then they shot us. I felt a fierce blow and saw blood flowing from my chest. Abu Hassan, who was next to me, pulled me to the ground. He instructed me to lie there motionless and pretend I was dead.'

My mother looked at him in horror. 'You mean, they killed all the men in the lorry?'

Serhad nodded. 'They even walked around to check if anyone was still alive. But I stayed absolutely still until they . . . until they brought the next lorry load of men – and shot them too.'

My mother let out a muffled scream. And I knew what this meant too: ISIS had systematically murdered all the men in our village.

'At that moment I made a run for it,' Serhad continued. 'Three other figures got up from the mountain of corpses at the same time. We ran for our lives.'

My two young brothers looked at him, distraught. 'So all the others were dead?' little Keniwar asked to make sure.

'All apart from us four boys,' Serhad confirmed. It took the two of them a moment to register what his words meant. Then they started to cry. They'd been so excited about seeing their father and older brothers again. It was a terrible shock for them, and for my mother too, of course.

'My poor husband, my poor son,' she said over and over again, as tears ran down her sunken cheeks. I squeezed her hand and felt utterly helpless. 'Oh, Farida,' she wept, 'I've basically known this from the day those thugs separated us. But I'd always kept a tiny crumb of hope.'

She told me how she herself had come to be imprisoned with the boys. 'I was holding their hands when the men pushed us out into the playground. All of us were terrified because we'd heard the shots. We thought it was our turn next. The buses and pickups were already back outside the playground, waiting for us.'

'An ISIS man pulled me away from you,' I recalled.

'Yes – and you looked at me with such fear in your eyes. It broke my heart that I couldn't do anything for you . . .'

'He said he'd invite us girls to dinner . . .'

'Yes, my poor child. But we all knew he was lying, didn't we?'

She sobbed. And I couldn't talk any more either. Silent tears ran down my face. My mother gently stroked my head.

'After they'd taken me to Tal Afar, they wanted to take Shivan away from me too,' she said, eventually continuing her story. All the boys were being groomed by ISIS for military training,' she told us.

Sometimes he was away for several days and she'd been terribly worried about him. 'They indoctrinated the boys. They tried turning them into Muslims. But whenever Shivan came back I told him he mustn't believe anything these criminals said . . . Isn't that right?'

She looked at Shivan. He nodded and now took up the thread. 'I kept asking, "Where's my mum?" And they replied, "Forget your parents; they're dead. We're your new family." But I knew they were lying.'

'My poor brother,' I said.

'They also forced us to read the Quran and pray to their God. But I only pretended to join in. I never really prayed to their God.'

'You did brilliantly.'

'Mum often said that Keniwar and I were ill, and couldn't take part in the training.'

'But then they said they were taking all the boys to Syria to fight,' my mother said. 'And I knew that it was time to run away before it was too late.'

One night when it was foggy they'd chanced an escape with some other women and their children. Together they got past the trenches ISIS had excavated around the village. They ended up in the middle of a battle zone where they were eventually rescued by the Peshmerga fighters. 'For us women our own survival wasn't important,' my mother said. 'The key thing was that the boys escaped before they were killed on the battlefield.'

'I'm very proud of you,' I said to all three of them. 'I'm proud to have such a brave family.'

My brothers Shivan and Keniwar came back with us to the camp and they also stayed with my uncle. On the advice of the doctors my mother was to remain in hospital for the time being. She was still too weak and needed feeding up. I visited her every day, because I didn't want to be without her for another second. I was so happy to have a mother again.

Then Mum was discharged and the camp management gave us our own container. As we now constituted a family again we had the right to a little space of our own. Although all of us were painfully aware that we were no longer a complete family, we were at least the remains of a family. When I stood between my mother and brothers on the container steps at daybreak each morning to greet the first rays of the sun, I felt that my place was among them. I never wanted to be without them again.

But then I received some news I hadn't been counting on. One sunny day Evin came running over to our container, waving papers she'd been given by the camp management. 'Farida, Farida!' she cried. 'We've been chosen.'

'Chosen for what?' I didn't grasp what she was saying.

'You know, for the programme in Germany. Don't you remember? The thing we applied for.'

'Oh, right!' All of a sudden I knew what she was talking about and, to be honest, I was a little shocked. 'Does that mean we can go to Germany now?'

'Yes, they're going to send us tickets, maybe even this month. We've got to get passports as quickly as we can.'

'But –'

'No buts!'

'But my mum's only just arrived!'

'Farida,' Evin said, taking my hand in hers, 'this is our chance. The opportunities for us in Germany are so much better. There's peace there. People are desperate to go. We have a duty to our families to take advantage of this opportunity, my uncle says.'

I thought long and hard about this. What did my friend mean by 'duty'? I couldn't imagine my family giving it the seal of approval if I planned to travel without them. That evening I talked to my brother Serhad and my mother. I was almost ashamed to put the idea to Mum. I was worried that she'd feel offended. But her reaction was unexpectedly composed.

'There's no future for us in Kocho any more,' she said. 'How could we live there after all that's happened? We'd never feel safe again.'

'Life's meant to be better in Germany,' Serhad said. 'All my new friends dream of emigrating there. A few of them are prepared to pay lots of money and make perilous journeys just to get there. If you're handed the opportunity you can't say no.'

I was quite bewildered. 'What about you?'

'We'll join you later,' Serhad said, half in jest, half serious. 'It won't take long.'

My mother nodded. 'Yes, Farida, take this opportunity,' she urged me. 'Maybe you can start a new life there.' She looked at me insistently. 'There's no fresh start here, you know that. People are too caught up in their old ways of thinking. And we'll never make peace with the Muslims . . .'

I was unsure. Did she really mean that? Was she actually trying to convince me to leave my family, my homeland and the place where the Seven Angels met every autumn? 'Are you really advising me to go?' I checked.

'Yes I am, Farida. I'm advising you and Evin and all the girls who were imprisoned to go.'

I lowered my eyes. Mother was talking about our stigma. Here in Iraq I knew it would follow us around forever. 'Maybe I could finish school in Germany,' I thought out loud, 'and study maths . . .' Later, when Kocho was liberated, I could always come back and work there as a maths teacher.

'Go,' my mother said firmly. 'The Lord will hold His hand above you and protect you as He has always done.'

EPILOGUE

Since summer 2015 I've been living in Germany. It's only four hours by plane from Erbil, in the north-east of Iraq. But the two countries inhabit different worlds: one at war, the other at peace. You'd think I'd have been delighted finally to go somewhere at peace. But adapting to this new, strange world has not been a simple process for me. Evin has found it similarly hard. And unfortunately we weren't allocated to the same town, which meant we couldn't be together any more. But we call each other on the phone and let each other know our news.

In Germany everything is different: the weather, the food, the smells, but particularly the people. The social workers who picked me up from the airport took me to a small town in this northern country. A pretty, but very unfamiliar town. To begin with I was accommodated with some other girls in a convent. It was very touching the way the nuns looked after us. And although their faith is very unlike ours, they didn't object in the slightest to us performing our own religious rituals and saying our prayers. They even encouraged us in this, I expect because they know what a huge support religion can be. They signed me up for a German course and invited me to discuss my experiences with a psychologist. I wasn't keen at first; I thought it would be better to forget what had happened. I wanted to leave all the horror in the past. But it haunted me in Germany too, for of course I carry it within me.

It was only after the first few sessions that I realised it did me good to talk, even if it wasn't always nice. In some mysterious way the conversations unravelled a knot inside me. Finally I was able to cry. Finally I could mourn for my dead ones, and for myself. I mourn for everything I have lost and left behind. And sometimes I feel very tired, so tired that I don't know whether I've got the strength to go on.

But then I decide that my life *will* go on, in spite of all the terrors. I won't give my tormentors the victory of having destroyed it. I'm back at school now; I really ought to be in year 12, but as my German's not perfect yet I've decided to repeat year 11. I'm already the best in the class at maths, but it's easier for me because I know all the material already! The teachers and my classmates are all terribly good to me, but they live such different lives, so easy-going.

After I'd been in the convent for a few weeks Mum called me with some news that brought tears to my eyes: she and my brothers were coming over to Germany! They'd submitted applications to emigrate and these had been approved. We have since been reunited. After my family arrived we were given a small apartment where we now all live together. I'm profoundly grateful to be able to be with my family again. The nuns were incredibly kind to us, but nobody can replace your own flesh and blood. And I'm also delighted that we can cook for ourselves again. I don't really like German food. Now my mother and I take turns to cook the dishes we know and love. The food and the aroma of the spices bring a hint of home to our apartment.

But I don't have much time for household chores. I'm now responsible for my family. And when I'm not at school or doing homework, I'm paying visits to the authorities. I've developed a pretty good understanding of German. I still find it difficult to talk, but if the other people don't speak too quickly and don't use dialect, I can now follow their conversations reasonably well.

We refugees continue to be treated well by the authorities and we're under a specific protection programme. I don't really like to think about what that means, but the places where we live are kept secret. We're not allowed to tell anyone and the authorities don't give the information out to anybody either. And this was even before the terrible attacks in Paris, Nice and Berlin demonstrated that the men who tortured me and others, and who killed our fathers and brothers, are now murdering people in Europe too.

When I've finished school in Germany, I'll study to become a maths teacher as I've always wanted to. The fanatics who degraded us and treated us like objects are not going to stop me pursuing this goal. I survived to prove to them that I'm stronger than they are.

CO-WRITER'S NOTE

It is early spring 2015 but a biting wind is still blowing through the streets in the Yazidi refugee camp near Dohuk. People live crowded together in containers, one family to each of these rectangular, single-room billets arranged in rank and file. Many of them house half a dozen people in twelve square metres. You can't keep any secrets here. Not from the neighbours, either, who are only separated by a poorly soundproofed wall. All the camp inhabitants know the stories that each of them would like to erase from their memory. But there is no forgetting here: forty kilometres from the territory still occupied by 'Islamic State' the trauma remains ever-present, hanging over the container city like an invisible toxic cloud.

I have been sent here by my editor to look for survivors of this nightmare. As a journalist I'm always interested in the viewpoints of women who get caught up in conflicts through no fault of their own; the viewpoints of the victims of male violence. I want to give them a voice.

I learn of what happened to Farida from a social worker. When I ask after her in the camp it's clear that people there know who she is. 'Farida escaped captivity only a few weeks ago, together with a group of girls,' they say, pointing the way to her uncle's container. By the door I meet a pale young woman whose hair is tied back with a scarf. Farida scrutinises me with her serious brown eyes. Sceptically at first, I get the impression. But then she smiles. No, I think, you can't tell at first glance what this nineteen-year-old has been through.

Farida invites me into her temporary home. Inside the container the gas stove gives out a little heat; I'm very glad to escape the wind outside. Several women are sitting on mattresses arranged in a rectangle along the walls: Farida's aunt, her four-year-old cousin, a few neighbours and her friend Evin. Farida serves me very sweet, hot tea and we quickly enter into conversation. It's not till a few glasses later that I venture to ask the young woman about her experiences as a prisoner of ISIS. Farida tentatively clears her throat. Then she starts talking, talking about the day her home village of Kocho was attacked and about her odyssey through the prisons of the ISIS realm. I can plainly see how difficult it is for her to articulate all this.

It's a major effort for her to talk. Sometimes she really has to force herself to answer my questions. But she's made her decision: she wants the world to find out what they did to her and the other girls. She wants to scream out the injustice. And yet she comes across as terribly distant. It seems as if she's put up an invisible wall, a protective wall between her and her experiences. The other women in the room appear absent too, betraying little emotion. Each of them is struggling with her own demons. Only occasionally do I hear one of them sigh, asking sadly, 'How could that have happened?'

When we meet the next time the sun is shining on the living containers. Farida is pleased to see me again, pleased about my interest in her, and she greets me like a friend with a kiss on the cheek. She has agreed for me to write a book based on her account. Now she wants to tell me her story in all its details. But this time without anyone else present. She asks all her relatives to leave us alone in the container so we can talk undisturbed. Not even her mother, who herself has returned from imprisonment since my last visit, is allowed to stay. Only a young Kurdish girl of Farida's age remains to help out with the translation, as I don't speak Kurdish, and Farida would prefer to talk in her mother tongue.

Farida starts by talking about her village, Kocho, about her family and the beautiful house they used to live in. She has a dreamy smile on her lips and she revels in these memories. She finds it very important to tell me about how her life was before the terrorists struck. Thanks to digital technology there are even a few photographs preserved from that time; on her mobile Farida shows me her favourite brother, the eldest. 'We were a perfectly normal family,' she says, faltering. All of a sudden tears flood her eyes, which seems to come as a shock to her; the first crack has appeared in her hard shell.

The longer we talk, the more distressing the interview becomes for Farida. Then we speak about places she associates with torture, and people who inflicted interminable suffering on her. It's an extremely painful process to recall these monsters, utter their names and describe them to me. Sometimes she reacts depressively, sometimes she gets furious. And time and again she complains about terrible headaches. Then she needs a break and I go for a walk in the camp with the translator so Farida can be on her own. We only resume when she gives the sign that it's all right. And so we painstakingly work our way through her memories, one agonising step after another.

The horror of her story, and the pain that talking about it unleashes in her again, leaves its mark on me too. Thanks to her highly detailed account I am able to imagine vividly the sinister world she describes. Soon I'm tormented by nightmares. Dreams in which I can clearly picture the scenes which she must have experienced and suffered. I think Farida senses that I'm suffering alongside her, and I get the impression that this affords her some comfort.

By the end of the interview we're both exhausted. I know it's going to take Farida a long time to process these horrific events and accept them as part of her biography, of her self. But an initial step has been taken and the conversations we've had are having an effect. We don't know when we'll see each other again. Farida has applied to go to Germany under the Baden-Württemberg programme and is waiting for her request to be approved. We embrace as we say goodbye.

'I'll think about you every day,' I promise her.

And I do. When I'm back home in Berlin, writing Farida's story, she's with me permanently. Each day, while fastidiously committing every detail to paper, inside my head, I'm living through all the horrors inflicted on Farida.

Often, after hours at my desk, it feels very strange to go back out into the world and continue with my normal life. Farida never had such breaks from her torture. How agonising it must have all been for her. Despite my intense engagement with her experiences in ISIS captivity I can only begin to imagine what she's gone through.

A few months later Farida is finally able to go to Germany, staying at first with Catholic nuns. Soon afterwards her mother and younger brothers obtain visas too. I'm delighted that all the surviving members of the family are now together and in safety. Will they manage to settle in their new home and leave behind the horrors they experienced in Iraq?

To begin with, Farida, at least, is struggling. She seems unhappy in her new life. When we speak on the phone she is uncommunicative. And that's not simply because she's only just started learning German. Now that the immediate danger has passed and she has some inner peace, she is sinking into post-traumatic depression.

Her first winter in Germany is an endurance test. In the grey days and long nights she is visited by the demons of her past. And nobody can protect her from them, not even me. I'd love to be able to help her, but I'm powerless against her inner torment.

As a symbol of her grief Farida is now wearing black. On her left arm she tattoos with needles and ink the names of her dead father and eldest brother. She also scratches Arabic letters on her fingers, which when she clenches her fist form the name of her village back home: 'Kocho'. In a book she lists all the names of the villagers from Kocho who were murdered. It's her way of mourning.

When our book is published during this period, Farida is imprisoned in the darkness of her damaged soul. Which is why she's not in a position to do the interviews we'd originally planned. And she doesn't want to see her photo on the cover of the book either. The publishing house and journalists respect her wishes and leave her in peace.

But her retreat leaves me feeling sad. Where's the brave girl I met in Iraq? I wonder. Where is Farida's fighting spirit, where is her courage? Have the terrorists succeeded in defeating her in the end? Such thoughts break my heart. 'Those men have caused enough misery,' I appeal to her, as I've so often done. 'Don't allow them any more power over you!' It's a hopeless attempt to encourage her. But my words aren't getting through. Farida insists on her isolation, her grief. And I can do nothing but give her the time she needs for this.

Farida doesn't get in touch until the summer, leaving me a brief message on my voicemail. To my surprise I realise that she can now speak almost perfect German. But more importantly her voice sounds different, oddly self-assured.

When we talk Farida tells me that she has thought everything through and is now ready to appear in public. 'Show your face, do you mean?' I ask in astonishment. For when we last spoke Farida was having none of it. She and her mother were almost more afraid of the social stigma within the Yazidi community in Germany than of possible reprisals from ISIS. 'So you no longer have any reservations?'

'No, I don't want to hide any more,' Farida says with determination.

'What about your family? Are they agreed?'

'My mother and brothers are completely behind me in this,' she says. 'They all think that as Yazidis we have a duty to let the world know about what happened to our people. My father would have wanted that too.' And then she asks something that makes me proud: 'Will you come with me?'

'Of course,' I assure her.

Shortly afterwards we meet up in the Netherlands. When we finally see each other again in a hotel in Amsterdam we fly into each other's arms. 'I'm so proud you've decided to take this step,' I whisper in her ear. 'It's so, so brave of you. I always knew that you were the bravest girl in the world.' She nods with tears in her eyes.

Farida has discarded her black clothes. In jeans and trainers, she now looks like any normal young European, perhaps a Greek girl. Her long dark hair is held up with a hair clip. But when the journalists and photographers arrive she's nervous. As Farida's story has met with particular interest in the Netherlands, all the major newspapers have sent their correspondents; the television cameras are there too.

'Stay calm,' I tell her. 'And if they ask you a question you don't want to answer, just give me a sign.'

'OK – deal,' she whispers, taking my hand.

Then it begins. She's hesitant with her responses at first, but then the answers become more fluent. She shows the press the book in which she wrote the names of the murdered people of Kocho during the long winter. 'It's not just about me and what happened to me,' she explains. 'It's about all these people. I want the crimes committed against us to be tried in a court of law.'

The journalists ask her how she's dealing with the social stigma of having been sexually assaulted. Farida looks at me and says nothing for a moment. Should I intervene? No, her eyes tell me. 'I don't have to be ashamed of anything,' she then says confidently. I squeeze her hand and just want to hug her there and then. I'm so pleased that she can finally see it this way too.

In the two years that we've known each other Farida has made such rapid progress. She's learned to accept that the violence inflicted on her is part of her story. Yes, it's taken time, but ultimately Farida has won the fight against ISIS and can live her life with her head held high again.

Essentially, she has defeated the terrorists twice. Once by escaping their physical violence. And the second time by banishing the terror from her head. This battle was perhaps the more difficult of the two.

It's been a great honour for me to be able to help her in this.

penguin.co.uk/vintage